Adventures with a
YORKSHIRE
VET

Lambing Time
and other Animal Tales

JULIAN NORTON

WALKER
BOOKS

First published 2022 by Walker Books Ltd
87 Vauxhall Walk, London SE11 5HJ

2 4 6 8 10 9 7 5 3 1

Text © 2022 Julian Norton
Illustrations © 2022 Jo Weaver
Photo © Julian Norton

The right of Julian Norton and Jo Weaver to be identified as author and illustrator
respectively of this work has been asserted in accordance with the Copyright,
Designs and Patents Act 1988

This book has been typeset in Miju Goudy

Printed and bound by CPI Group (UK) Ltd, Croydon, CR0 4YY

British Library Cataloguing in Publication Data:
a catalogue record for this book is available from the British Library

ISBN 978-1-5295-0998-4

www.walker.co.uk

CONTENTS

FOREWORD

WHEN I WAS A SMALL BOY, on Sunday evenings at about six o'clock, my family and I would sit down to watch *All Creatures Great and Small* on television. The programme was based on the books of James Herriot, a vet working in rural North Yorkshire in the 1930s. Like so many future vets of my generation, I was captivated. Becoming a vet became my dream.

Some years later, in pursuit of that dream, I arrived at a veterinary practice in the Yorkshire Dales, eager and ready to learn the ropes. I thrust out my hand towards the senior partner, hoping to make a good impression.

"You've got cold hands," the vet bellowed. He was right. I'd just cycled ten miles on my bike without any gloves, through sleet and snow, to spend the first of five days with him and his colleagues.

"Don't take your coat off," he called as he strode out of the office. "We have some cows to see. Plenty of visits to make today, so we'd better crack on. And bring your wellies with you."

Despite my freezing fingers, I felt a surge of excitement as I hurried after him. I was about to get my first taste of what it might be like to be a vet. I remember the various shades of brown farmyards and cowsheds, and the warm moisture rising from the backs of the housed cattle, all lined up side by side. I can still smell the farmyard too – the breath of the cows, the fruity silage and the sweet hay. And I was mystified and fascinated by the vet as he examined every cow, proclaiming the exact details of the goings-on of each one. *How does he know these things?* I wondered.

But as much as I recall the veterinary skills and the animals' ailments, I mostly remember the people. The farmers, whose weather-worn faces all had their own stories to tell. Of course, every farm animal has someone who cares for them and, some years later, once I'd made it through vet school and out into the world as a veterinary surgeon, I realized that treating an animal was only half the job. It is great fun, endlessly challenging, satisfying and rewarding. But it is the people and their stories that really make the life of a vet extra special.

The ten stories in this book give you a glimpse into the world of both the people and their animals in the part of Yorkshire where I've been lucky enough to have lived and worked. I hope you enjoy these tales and I hope they inspire the same love and understanding of animals that have captivated me since I was a child.

Julian

Poor Pigley!

The little practice nestled under the gentle Yorkshire hills was the place where my veterinary career really began. As a student, I'd dreamt of spending my days working with and helping animals. Now, having passed my exams and graduated from veterinary school, I could, at last, live that dream.

My first couple of weeks at the practice had been particularly busy and it was quickly becoming clear to me that I was going to have my hands full. Every time I stepped into the waiting room, there were new patients arriving and each one seemed to present a different challenge.

It was another hectic morning at the practice when Pigley the micro-pig arrived. The dogs, cats and rabbits felt quite at ease as they waited their turn to be seen, but Pigley's arrival caused some alarm, because most of the animals had never seen a pig before. They viewed Pigley with fascination and some suspicion.

Pigley quickly made himself at home in the packed waiting room, investigating and snuffling around, sniffing dogs and making small, contented grunting noises to himself. A cat in a basket hissed when he oinked at it, causing him to make a high-pitched squeal.

I chuckled. "Looks like another normal day at the practice," I said to Emmy, my loyal

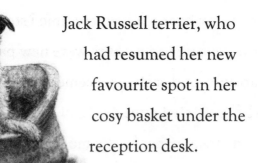

Jack Russell terrier, who had resumed her new favourite spot in her cosy basket under the reception desk.

At one point, a pug approached Pigley, sniffed him and started barking frantically, his eyes bulging even more than usual. The pug was called Ffion. He was recovering from a broken leg, which I'd repaired with a plate and some screws during my first week at the practice. The round little dog still had a cumbersome blue bandage on his leg, which we were planning to remove during his appointment – my final job before I turned my attention to Pigley.

Usually, farm animals are treated on the farm. It's impossible to bring a cow to the vet's and difficult to fetch a horse, although occasionally people ride their horse to the surgery and wait in the car park to be seen. But small farm animals – such as baby micro-pigs, lambs or pygmy goats – are portable enough to bring along, just like a dog. Once, I treated a miniature Mediterranean donkey at the practice. It arrived on the back seat of a car!

I headed back into my consulting room, watching Pigley and Ffion through the long, thin window in the door. After a hesitant start, the two sausage-shaped creatures seemed to have struck up an unlikely friendship. Ffion wiggled vigorously from side to side as he tried to wag his tail, but since it was curled in a tight corkscrew, it didn't really wag like a normal dog's tail. Instead, his whole body wagged. When he ventured close to Pigley, he barked and then jumped back, curious but cautious. He repeated the process over and over again, desperate to become friends, but unsure what Pigley was and whether he might attack. *What is this curious creature?* he must have been thinking.

Pigley sniffed at the big blue bandage on Ffion's leg. This was the first pug the pig had ever seen and Pigley was fascinated by its blue leg. Every time Ffion barked, Pigley grunted, almost causing the astonished pug's eyes to pop out of his head with surprise! Pigs spend most of their time grunting, as they are interested in what's going on around them. They are silent only when they are asleep.

I called Ffion into my room and hoisted him onto the table. Despite everything he had been through at the surgery in recent weeks, he was always pleased to see me. I leant in to stroke his cheery face and he immediately stood on his hind legs, licking my face and ears, as if telling me all about the strange animal he had just encountered in the waiting room. I gently unravelled the bandage. Underneath, the leg looked excellent. The wound was clean and healed, the broken bone now firm and already strong. I smiled to myself. *Not bad for a new vet*, I thought.

"Good news, Ffion," I said as I popped him back on the floor. "I'll be able to leave this leg without a bandage on. It's healing very nicely." His owners looked delighted. "You should come back for a check-up in two weeks," I continued. "Take it easy and DON'T jump off the sofa again. Remember, pugs can't fly!"

Pigley looked as surprised as a pig could be when his new friend emerged from the consulting room with a different-coloured leg. The new one was thinner and no longer blue. Maybe that was why Pigley was anxious when I called for him and his owner, Joyce, to come in. But it wasn't his leg I'd be looking at. Pigley had a poorly eye.

"Good morning," said Joyce as she and Pigley stepped into the room. "This is Pigley. He's just four weeks old. He's going to be part of our family at Beech Tree Farm.

He lives in the house and has a bed by the large stove in the kitchen. He's very intelligent and clever and sociable, and he'll fit in very well with the other animals. But he has a sore eye that's bothering him. He's rubbing it on the carpet and even squinting. It looks painful."

Joyce was quite right. Pigley's eye was indeed rather sore and it needed sorting out. Treating an infected eye is simple in the case of a dog or a cat or even a guinea pig as they are fairly docile. But when it comes to a pig, the process is much more difficult. Keeping the pesky pig still, so I could examine the eye properly, was the first challenge.

Pigs – even tiny, friendly ones that live in a house and have just befriended a small dog in the waiting room – make a massive fuss about doing things that they don't want to do. They cannot be persuaded. If they are put in a situation that they don't want to be in, they will squeal and squeal very loudly in protest. The noise is high-pitched and more intense than anything that comes out of the mouth of any other animal.

The volume of the squealing often bears no relation to the degree of discomfort or inconvenience that this pig is experiencing. Whether something terrible has just happened, or whether another pig has just looked at them in slightly the wrong way, the dramatic reaction is the same. I suspected this would be the case with Pigley. I scooped him up from Joyce's arms and carried him, wrapped snuggly in a blanket, to the prep area in the middle of the practice, where I could get help from one of the nurses.

"Right, this is Pigley," I started to explain to Lucy the nurse. "He's very friendly and has already made friends with Ffion in the

waiting room. Poor Pigley, he has a sore eye.
I need to keep him still, examine it and work
out what to do. It won't hurt him, but I'm
certain he will make a huge noise, whatever
I try. So be prepared."

In some circumstances, people working
with pigs even wear ear defenders. Would we
need some today? I hoped not. Lucy clutched
Pigley firmly. Sure enough, Pigley emitted
ear-splitting squeals every time I went near
him – before I'd even done anything. The
anticipation was more frightening to him
than the actual procedure. Squeals echoed
around every corner of the practice. Luckily,
I couldn't see the reaction of the other
animals in the waiting room, or their owners'
responses. I just hoped Ffion had already left
the building!

"Stay still, Pigley," I implored. "I haven't
done anything yet!" It was true. So far, Lucy

was keeping him still – or trying to – as I pointed a small torch into his tiny piggy eye. Eventually, I managed to get a brief glimpse, then apply some special orange-coloured drops to the eye to check for damage. This caused more noises and more complaining from Pigley, even though it was not in the least uncomfortable. I often use these drops for examining eyes. They make everything go orange and I often wonder what a patient must think when their vision completely changes colour.

"Don't worry, Pigley," I said. "The orange colour will soon pass. It's completely normal."

He shrieked again, unable to understand. After Pigley had got used to the orange drops, and after we'd stopped shining lights at him, Pigley's noise levels subsided. I used a moist cotton wool swab to gently bathe the area. Even with pleasantly warm water, Pigley screeched and squealed. I wondered what his reaction would have been if the water had been cold. Pigley didn't know how lucky he was.

"Pigley! Shhhhhhh!" we all cried, but Pigley wouldn't shush. The final treatment was some ointment. You can imagine what Pigley thought of that!

Finally, he calmed down and nestled his bullet-shaped head into the crook of Lucy's arm, where it was dark, comfy, warm and safe. The whole noisy process took less than five minutes. Pigley's ordeal was over and he wiggled back to the room where Joyce had been waiting.

"He's all done," I announced. "It went very smoothly, very simply and, contrary to what you might think judging by the noise level, without any discomfort at all!" I added reassuringly. From her experience with pigs, I knew Joyce believed me, although many of my other patients wouldn't have! "He'll need more treatment each day and it might be better if we do it. He's quite a handful."

Over the next few days, Pigley visited us for more ointment to be applied to his poorly eye. Each time he squealed and squealed but the infection was gradually improving.

After that, Joyce visited the practice every so often with her other animals, and she was always sure to update me on Pigley. He had settled well into his home at Beech Tree Farm. She showed me pictures of him living in the kitchen, in his fluffy bed next to the stove. She told me stories of him lying on her bed upstairs, relaxing and sometimes snoring, or of how he played football in the garden and thought he was one of the dogs. Of course, Pigley had grown, like all micro-pigs do, because they don't stay tiny for ever, but he was enjoying life as part of the extended family of animals down on the farm.

One morning, Joyce called me out of the blue. I could instantly hear the worry in her voice. "It … it's Pigley. He … he's been trodden on by a horse," she stammered, clearly very upset.

My first thought was *How on Earth has that happened? Pigley lives in the kitchen. Has Joyce now got a horse in the kitchen too?* I asked some questions, trying to calm Joyce down and find out more about what had happened.

"One of our horses stood on him by accident. It wasn't her fault – she didn't know he was there. And one of his feet has been really damaged. And what a noise! I can still hear the squeals!"

It turned out that the accident had happened in the field, when Pigley was out for a walk after breakfast. I also found out that Joyce hadn't been able to apply any sort of bandage, because Pigley kept running away and making loud, objecting noises. When he wasn't running away from Joyce, Pigley returned to his bed and tried to rest. His poor foot was bleeding badly. It was very clear that this was an emergency.

"Don't worry. I'm on my way," I said quickly. I gathered a box of bandages, whistled to Emmy and headed out.

I had only been at the practice for a short while and I was still finding my veterinary feet as well as my way around the rolling hills and small farms of North Yorkshire.

Beech Tree Farm was quite a long way away, right at the edge of the Yorkshire Dales. Emmy jiggled about on the front seat of the car as we drove through the bumpy country lanes and over a few potholes.

"Sorry, Em," I said as the car bounded along. I rushed as fast as I could, picturing the complete chaos that lay ahead of us. Pigley had reacted dramatically to a very simple and relatively painless procedure when he was just a few weeks old. With something much more painful and without anything to numb the damaged area, he would be inconsolable. I hoped I'd be able to help.

A sorry sight awaited us in the kitchen when we arrived at Joyce's farm. Two Labradors lay calmly in their own beds under the kitchen table, but Pigley limped around, pushing the affected leg out to the side so he could take weight on the inside of his foot without putting the damaged outer foot on the ground. Pigs, like sheep and cows, have two toes on each foot.

As soon as I walked in, Pigley scuttled as best he could under the table, to hide next to the dogs. I signalled to Emmy to wait by the door, which she did obediently, settling down on the stone floor.

I'm sure Pigley recognized me as the horrible man who had peered into his little eyes only a few weeks ago. He was definitely not going to come and greet me today.

"Hello, Pigley," I said, crouching down. "What's happened to your foot? Are you going to let me have a look at it?"

Pigley was much bigger now and he grunted disapprovingly at me from under the table and stubbornly refused to come out. Even from some distance away, I could see that the foot looked a horrible mess. I immediately knew that I'd have to try and apply a bandage to stop the bleeding and protect the delicate surface. I'd need to keep

Pigley still somehow. I'd learnt from plenty
of other patients (though mainly dogs, like
Ffion) that applying a bandage to a moving
target was almost impossible.

"Joyce, I'll need to put a bandage on
Pigley's foot," I explained. "I don't think
there will be anything broken – if that was
the case, he wouldn't be able to put any
weight on it at all. But it must be terribly sore,
and we need to stop the bleeding. Can we

tempt him out from under the table and keep him still whilst I apply the bandage?"

"Oh yes. He'll do anything for an apple, or even a piece of toast," said Joyce. "And once he's out, I'm sure he'll take himself off to his own bed. That's our best chance," she added hopefully.

Two slices of bread were placed in the toaster, and we waited. As soon as they popped up, Pigley heard the noise and sniffed the homely toasted smell. He waddled out, making the happy grunting noise that a hungry pig makes when it thinks food is about to be served.

"Well done, Pigley," Joyce said, rubbing the bulky pig behind his ears. "Here's your second breakfast. Why don't you eat it in bed, you poor thing?"

Sure enough, Pigley carried one of the pieces of toast to his very comfy-looking bed. He chewed it and Joyce quickly offered him the other piece.

"He likes two pieces of toast," she explained. I half expected them to be smothered in butter and marmalade!

When I was at university, a wise and experienced professor taught us that the secret to success with a pig is to use stealth. Gentle, quiet movements, soothing words, rubs behind the ears or on the tummy were all good tactics. Sudden movements, surprises, needles, cold water or stingy antiseptic would all cause pig anxiety.

Pigley lay in his bed, sleepy after his toast and relaxed from the warmth of the large kitchen stove. I readied myself with bandages and knelt next to him.

"Good Pigley, what a brave pig," I said, rubbing his tummy with one hand as I lined up the first layer of bandage material, which was a smooth and protective pad.

Joyce added more encouragement, scratching his ears. I took a deep breath and gently applied the pad over the wound, desperately hoping he wouldn't react and run back under the table. We praised him more loudly as it touched his sore skin. Pigley stayed still and made contented little grunts, so far apparently unaware I was fiddling with his injured foot. Stage one complete!

I had two more layers to apply, so there was still some way to go.

The second layer was a soft cotton wool bandage, which would provide comfort as well as keep the pad in position. This was crucial and often the time when animals might pull away.

"What a good pig!" we both said, getting louder and louder with each turn of the bandage. Pigley seemed to be relishing the compliments and extra fuss. He made no attempt to withdraw his foot, which was nothing short of a miracle. I recalled how violently he'd reacted to my intervention when we'd first met and felt sure he would remember and be totally uncooperative. But in the comfort of his own kitchen with a warm bed and his favourite snacks, and with the benefit of him being a little older, he was being very grown-up!

The last layer was a stretchy protective material, which was essential to keep everything together and firmly in place. As I took it out of the package, I suddenly realized that it was exactly the same blue colour as the bulky bandage I'd removed from Ffion's leg when Pigley had met him at the practice on that noisy day.

With Pigley still relaxed, I wound the blue material round and round, extending it higher up Pigley's leg. It was neat and tidy and I was very pleased Pigley had stayed put for long enough to get the dressing on properly. It looked superb and would provide the important protection needed to allow the injury to heal.

"You'll have to keep it dry, if possible," I explained to Joyce as I admired my work. "If he's going outside in the wet or the mud, put a plastic bag over the bandage to protect it."

But Pigley's patience had finally run out. He leapt up with a shriek and skulked back under the table. The leg obviously felt funny with the new bandage, but the relief was clear, as I'd expected.

What wasn't expected was his reaction when Pigley noticed the bright blue colour! To him, it obviously meant that what had happened to his friend Ffion was sure to happen to him. Next time, this vet would change his fat blue leg and swap it for a thin brown one! I tried to reassure him, but Pigley was already running out of the door.

I laughed. "Looks like he's already made a speedy recovery!"

We walked out into the bright, cold day, pausing for a moment while Joyce dutifully wrapped a plastic bag around Pigley's foot. Pigley grunted and then trotted happily around the farm, carrying on as if nothing had ever happened.

"Come on then, Em. Our work here is done." Emmy barked eagerly. She was ready to get back to the practice and see what the rest of the day had in store, and so was I.

Trouble for Duchess

By the end of my first month at the practice, I was finally starting to feel like I was settling into life as a vet in Yorkshire. Saturday morning surgery had gone by uneventfully, and during the afternoon I only had to deal with a dog with an upset stomach and a cat with a small wound on its foot. There was not even anything to interest Emmy, who was usually excited by everything. She snoozed lazily under the desk at reception.

In the quiet moments of the day, I'd checked and rechecked the equipment in the boot of my car, ensuring I had all I needed to cover any incident I might encounter. Then, late one Sunday night, the phone rang and everything changed.

"Towton here," came the booming voice down the line, so loudly that I had to move the receiver further away from my ear. "I have a problem with a cow," he bellowed. "She's just calved and pushed out her calf bed. I need a vet immediately."

A "calf bed out" is the phrase most farmers use to describe the condition where the womb – the place where the calf grows – accidentally comes out just after the calf is born. Returning it to its proper position inside the cow, often swollen, not to mention covered in straw, is one of the hardest jobs for a farm animal vet.

"OK, Mr Towton, I'll be right on my way," I replied. "Where exactly is your farm?"

"Ah," he said, "you're the new vet, aren't you? We're at Castle Farm – last turn before the castle off the road to Kirkham, on the right." And with that he was gone.

This was my chance to save a life and help an animal in distress, and I was ready. It was the first time I'd been called on to do this kind of procedure by myself, and I knew it would have been very tough for a vet at any stage of their career. I was nervous, but most of all, I felt excited, which is why I couldn't stop smiling. *This is why I've become a vet*, I kept thinking as I called to Emmy. Together we leapt into my car and headed out to Castle Farm.

As I followed the meandering roads towards the farm, I imagined the challenge that awaited me and what I might need to do to help my patient. This is a habit that has stayed with me for my whole career. I tried to picture the patient – would she be quiet and sleepy, lying tired after a long and difficult calving? Maybe she would be wild and impossible to catch? Either way, treating her was not going to be easy.

I imagined the people too. Already, from Mr Towton's few words over the phone, I had conjured up an image of him. He'd be tall, possibly wearing a deerstalker hat and tweeds. The briefness of the conversation suggested he might be rather ferocious.

Perhaps he was a "Sir" or a "Lord"?
If this was the case, there was bound to be
a farm manager too, or at least some sort of
extra help on hand.

"I wonder what Castle Farm is like?" I said
to Emmy, who cocked her head, listening
intently. "Maybe we're going to a castle, Em!"

I didn't have to wait long to find out.
The directions were simple to follow, and I
located the farm quickly. The fold yard where
the cattle were safely housed was illuminated
by a bright light above one of the doorways
and dim lights from a couple of nearby
outbuildings. It gave everything a yellowy-
orange hue and cast long shadows. It was a
dark and chilly night, and there was nobody
around when I arrived. I parked the car, then
pulled on my wellies and waterproof trousers.

"Right," I said, turning to Emmy, who was
sitting next to me on the passenger seat,

her tail wagging. "Things might get tricky
this evening, so I think you should stay in the
car for this one."

Emmy sat quietly and obediently as ever.
"Good girl. Be back soon," I said. "Wish me
luck, Em." If only she could talk, I'm sure she
would have.

Mr Towton suddenly appeared from a
doorway, along with another person, their
shadows becoming visible before they did.
They must have heard me arrive and left the
stricken cow to greet me. As I strode towards
them, I could see that the farm owner was
very tall. Smoke billowed around him, then I

noticed his pipe, which was lodged between his left hand and his mouth. Plumes of bluish-grey smoke rose from it at a constant rate, like a steam train. His assistant, a shorter man, was the first one to talk when I approached them.

"Now then! You must be the vet'nary?" he said cheerfully. "I'm Shane, farm manager 'ere. Nice to meet you. She's in a bad way. I hope you're feeling strong!"

"Hello. Yes, I'm Julian. Nice to meet you. I believe you have a very special herd, so I'll be glad to help this evening," I said. I had heard about the cattle on this farm – they were renowned. The herd was one of the oldest and most established group of beef shorthorn cattle in the country. Knowing that the cattle were so valuable and sought-after brought an added sense of pressure. I knew I had to act quickly and decisively.

Shane chuckled. It was a friendly first meeting and I sensed that he was very used to working with young vets who were new at their job. I expected some gentle teasing and light-hearted fun, but I hoped he'd take me on my merits, although I wasn't so sure his boss would.

"And have you done many of these before?" asked Mr Towton, obviously anxious that the new vet might be totally lacking in experience.

"I have in veterinary school and I'm sure I can help your cow tonight, so please don't worry," I said, trying my best to appear confident. "Does she have a name?" I asked as we walked towards the barn.

"She's called Duchess," said Shane. "Well, technically she's Duchess III. 'Er grandmother was Duchess and 'er mother was Duchess II. She's from a great family.

I suppose that little one in the corner will be Duchess IV!" Shane moved aside to allow me to see into the gloomy calving pen. "She's in 'ere."

A little white calf was lying quietly in a corner, curled up like a sleeping dog. Mum was standing near by, looking rather sad, with her head down and ears drooping. As I got closer to her and walked around the barn, I could instantly see what the problem was. She had a huge swelling that almost reached down to the barn floor. It looked extremely painful. I put my hand on Duchess's back and rubbed her thick coat to try and comfort her as I worked out what to do.

I would need to try and clean the swollen womb as much as I could without causing further damage to the delicate tissue. Then I would somehow have to feed it back into poor Duchess without tearing it.

To make matters more difficult, as I did this Duchess's instincts would tell her that it was another calf and so she should push!

Despite Duchess's big problems, she had made a good start looking after her baby,

because the calf was already dry and clean from her licking – a strong maternal instinct that kicks in even if the mother isn't doing so well. It's one of the many reasons why I think animals are so amazing: they keep going, even in the face of extreme circumstances.

"OK," I said, and patted her back one more time. Then I turned to the farmer and his helper to explain my plan. "We'll have to fasten her to the wall with a halter. Then I'll give her an injection," I explained confidently. "It will numb the whole area so she doesn't feel anything and doesn't push so much. And I'll need a bucket of warm water and a clean, empty sack, please."

My strategy was met with blank faces and disbelief.

"I'm not sure about this injection thing," Mr Towton blurted out next, clearly alarmed by what sounded like a modern and complicated technique. "Your boss never does that sort of thing. Is it safe? This cow is one of the most valuable animals in the country, you know. She's from a long line of champions." Then he added, "I don't want anything to jeopardize her chances." He put great emphasis on the word "jeopardize".

I tried to explain that giving the injection would actually improve her chances by making the procedure more straightforward, but time was running out. Poor Duchess started mooing at an alarming rate and staggering on her feet. I had to act now. But first I had to administer the injection correctly – it had to work...

Shane went scuttling away to get the water and a halter and returned with everything, including a large, rough hessian cloth sack, once used for carrying oats or grain from the farm mill to the bull pens.

Duchess was quiet and suffering from the early stages of shock, so she didn't put up any resistance as we gently looped the halter over her head, behind her ears and under her chin. Shane secured it firmly around a wooden hay manger on the wall of the pen. It didn't look very strong, but I was confident he'd done this hundreds of times before.

I positioned myself behind Duchess and lightly snipped some hair off the top of her tail, where it joined her back. Then I swabbed her skin with some surgical spirit on a piece of cotton wool and drew up local anaesthetic into a syringe. I held the syringe between my teeth and used one hand to wiggle the tail up and down, as if I were pumping the handle of an old-fashioned well, while using the index finger of my other hand to feel for the exact point where the tail joined the spine.

If the syringe went into the perfect

place, the cow's tail would immediately go floppy, the area would go numb and my job, contrary to what Mr Towton thought, would be considerably easier. If it didn't hit the right place, it wouldn't work at all.

"Here goes," I said under my breath, hoping my nervousness was not too obvious. I thought of Emmy's happy face, willing me on from her comfy seat in the car. I took a couple of deep breaths, then it was done.

After a few seconds, I started wiggling Duchess's tail. SUCCESS! It was as soft as a rope and my heart skipped a beat with excitement.

"That's gone very well," I explained, trying not to be too triumphant at this early stage. "Look, the tail is slack, so it's worked a treat, and it'll make the next part a lot easier."

"Well I never," Mr Towton exclaimed between puffs on his pipe. I hadn't noticed, but its smoke had almost filled the calving pen, making a foggy haze.

I rinsed and washed the swollen calf bed with warm water, removing straw and debris. Duchess didn't feel any discomfort and didn't react at all, which made life much simpler.

"Good girl," I said to her reassuringly. "You're doing really well." Then I turned to the farmers. "We're making good progress. Right, I need you two to hold this sack on either side, lifting it when I say. It will make it easier to feed everything back into position," I told them with extra confidence.

"I'm not sure about that," said Mr Towton, expressing yet more doubt. "Your boss would always do this with the cow lying down. He finds it easier that way. Says the angle of the pelvis helps it slide back inside."

It was true. As I'd learnt from my days as a student, sometimes it's better to do this job on the ground, with both of the cow's legs pointing backwards like a frog. But this would involve casting the cow with ropes so she would lie down, which wasn't always simple. Tonight, I opted for the standing version. Even though Mr Towton remained unconvinced, I made my decision and set to work.

I swilled more tepid water over the swelling before applying a gel to the outside to help lubricate the calf bed. Next came the slow and painstaking attempts to push the calf bed back inside. Contrary to Mr Towton's prediction, it was never going to "slide" back in! I pushed gently and almost immediately felt like I was making progress.

"That's great. Can you lift up the edges of that sack, please? Just a bit higher," I panted.

It was already smaller by about a third, now the size of a large bag of shopping. *Any moment now*, I said to myself, more in hope than expectation.

But disaster struck almost as soon as the thought entered my head. Duchess let out a loud moo and shifted her stance, causing the calf bed to drop back to its initial hanging position. I was distraught.

"I really think we should do it like the one your boss did earlier in the year," Towton said, still sceptical about my plan.

"Well, I think it's working," Shane interjected supportively. "It was almost in until she moved."

We reset our positions and started again. By now, all the pushing and effort had caused Mr Towton's pipe to go out, which at least reduced the likelihood of me coughing from the smoke! Again, the edges of the calf bed went in quite smoothly and I regained my strength with the end in sight.

All of a sudden, the final portion fell inwards with a very satisfying *plop!*, like the noise you hear when the final swirling water from a bath disappears down the plughole.

Everyone was visibly delighted, including poor Duchess! To celebrate, Mr Towton refilled his pipe and ignited it with deep puffs, which immediately brought back the smoky atmosphere. I cleaned my arm, added a little gel, then reached in to check that everything was holding in place. I did a quick bit of stitching up, then stepped back.

Duchess returned to inspect her sleeping calf, wobbling over to the corner of the pen with her still-numb legs – the after-effects of my magical injection. I rinsed my hands, arms and upper body again, and prepared some more injections for her.

"She'll need some antibiotics to stop infection, some painkillers and a hormone injection," I explained.

"What about some calcium?" Mr Towton suggested. "Your boss always gives a whole bottle of calcium to cows like this. He says it's essential."

"That's a good idea," I agreed. A dose of calcium would help Duchess produce milk for her newborn.

I went back to the car to get one, chuckling that my night's work had been successful in many ways. I'd cured Duchess and made a good impression on an experienced farmer. I could tell that fitting into the traditional world of Yorkshire farming wouldn't be so easy and would take more than just one night's success. But I was happy I'd made a good start.

And Emmy was happy too! She wagged her tail, like a helicopter, as I approached. "It worked, Em!" I said to her, ruffling the tufty fur on her head. "I'm nearly done. The last job is a big injection for Duchess, then we can get home. I think we both need our tea!"

I headed back to the barn. Duchess was a little steadier on her feet and her calf was dozing happily in the soft hay. I climbed back into the calving pen and decanted the large brown bottle of calcium solution into a drip, as apparently all the old vets in the practice would do. As the liquid slowly trickled into Duchess, Mr Towton started talking to me about his herd.

"I have another cow, an old girl. She's losing condition. The other vets have all seen her and have no idea what's going on. Would you mind having a look at her? Perhaps you might have a suggestion or two, because it's certainly flummoxed everyone else."

"Of course," I agreed, barely able to hide my grin for the second time in the evening, delighted that I'd obviously made a positive impression. "I can come back in the morning to take a look at her for you."

I smiled to myself. This would be another chance for me to show this old farmer some of my more modern treatment methods that the other vets might not have thought to try.

A diagnosis would be required and it wouldn't be easy, but with Emmy by my side I felt ready to solve the mystery and help another animal in need.

A Tale of Two Greedy Alpacas

As November arrived, all the leaves had fallen from the trees. When I had first started at the practice, the Yorkshire countryside had looked at its beautiful best, with every shade of orange, brown and yellow that you could imagine on the steep slopes along the edge of the moors. Now, everything was bare and grey. Low mist hovered over the fields.

Out and about on my visits, the damp and cold seemed to get through every layer of extra clothing I added. There was special beauty in these darkest days, but it was a tough time of year to be outside, either as a vet or an animal.

Some animals cope better than others with a British winter. Cattle grow thick, tough winter coats, as do horses. Sheep have deep fleece all year round, which keeps them warm. The greasy lanolin in their wool repels water, so they stay dry, too. Of course, most lucky animals are brought inside, with barns and cowsheds providing shelter from the worst of the Yorkshire weather.

Other animals are not so lucky, or well adapted, though. Alpacas, newcomers to North Yorkshire, have the warmest coats of all, so they could easily cope with the cold, but what they lack is any proper waterproofing. In the high mountains of South America, where they come from, it is cold – much colder than the coldest day here – but not wet. So, on a damp day in early winter, they struggle. It's like wearing a warm fleece jacket but standing in the rain – no use at all. For this reason, all alpacas must have access to a shelter, so they can stay dry.

What alpacas don't need access to, however, is an unlimited supply of food. A wet and cold alpaca is hungry and desperate for extra food – just like a child would be after playing a football match in the rain. But whereas a young footballer may tuck into a bowl of hot porridge or a bacon sandwich to warm up, young and greedy alpacas must make do with alpaca food, which is less glamorous but just as nutritious.

And so, very early on a dark, cold, misty November morning, a group of greedy young alpacas decided they wanted extra food and ended up getting a lot more than they were bargaining for.

The quiet of the morning was interrupted by my pager buzzing . I turned to look at the bright screen, still half asleep, and read the panicked message: *Alpacas gorged on food and choking. Come quickly! Emergency! Jackie.*

Jackie was a local alpaca farmer and she was clearly really upset. I sat up groggily and called Jackie to reassure her.

"Morning, Jackie," I mumbled. "I'll be with you as soon as I can."

I was tired. The autumn had been very busy and there had been lots of nights on call. I was loving my job, working hard and gaining experience by the bucketload – on occasion, quite literally by the bucketload. But the long days and interrupted nights were starting to take their toll.

I wondered whether I could roll over and grab an extra few minutes' rest, but I didn't dare risk it – there was every possibility that if I did that, I would fall back into a deep sleep. So, I rubbed my eyes and dragged myself out of bed for the umpteenth time this autumn. I'd been so warm and cosy, and I knew it would be freezing outside. Worse still, there was no time for breakfast, not even a quick cup of tea, because this sounded like a real emergency.

In the kitchen, Emmy was in her bed. She, too, had been fast asleep, warm by the fire, which was still glowing. She was in the same position I'd left her last night, tucked under a fleecy blanket, but she lifted her head when she heard me.

"Are you coming, girl?" I asked optimistically. Emmy came with me pretty much everywhere I went on my rounds,

sitting on the passenger seat or sometimes on my lap. She liked being with me on my adventures but had also learnt that there was every chance of a walk – even if only a short one – after I'd finished my work on a farm. Despite the darkness, she jumped up, stretched and yawned, then followed me outside, scuttling to the car, desperate to get there first!

It was pitch-black when we left the house. It would be for a while. Thick mist had shrouded everything around, so the drive to Jackie's had to be slow. Although I knew the roads and this was an urgent call-out, I had to be careful. I didn't want to drive off the winding roads and crash into a hedge!

As I made my way through the fog, I pondered the problem awaiting me.

"Emmy, you'll never believe what we've got this morning!" I said out loud. "Some alpacas have stuffed themselves with food. That sounds like a proper midnight feast! Can you imagine?"

Emmy stared at me intently, concentrating hard to try and understand what I was saying.

Were the alpacas really choking? I couldn't work out how it had happened. Everything at Jackie's farm was so immaculate and secure, with strong gates and well-made doors. The hinges were oiled and didn't squeak, and the hooks and locks that kept everything closed worked perfectly.

There are many farms I've visited where gates are held together with a combination of old rope and optimism. On one farm I sometimes attended, the sheep would regularly escape because the hedges and fences were in such a poor state.

Also, the bedding in the cowsheds hadn't been cleaned out, which meant it was so deep that cattle could just step over the gate which was supposed to keep them inside. They'd walk to their freedom in the fields beyond.

But at Jackie's there was no such chance, because everything was in tip-top order. The food store was secure – a firmly closed door prevented animals entering from the barn – and the alpaca food was kept in a plastic barrel, which had a lid that was surely too sturdy for an animal to lift off. So how the young alpacas had managed to get out of their field and into the feed was anyone's guess.

When I finally arrived, Jackie was pacing around the yard anxiously. I parked right outside the barn from where a low light was shining out.

"You stay there, Em," I said, clambering out of the warm car into the chilly morning gloom.

"You can watch what I'm doing through the window."

Jackie raced up to me and quickly described the problem.

"I found them this morning. Somehow, they got into the food store. Then, between them, they lifted the lid off their food container and have eaten almost all of it. They're choking, Julian. The food has swollen up and it's spilling out of their mouths. Please help them!"

I hurried through the wide-open doors of the barn. Inside, the young alpacas were looking very sorry for themselves. One was standing, coughing and drooling. Another was lying on the ground, head and neck extended, gasping for breath. This was the one to which I turned my attention first and quickly started my assessment. Mushy liquid feed was spilling out of its mouth and nose, making it almost impossible for the poor animal to breathe.

"This one's Geronimo," Jackie said, wiping his nose and stroking his head affectionately. "What do you think? He's bad, isn't he? What can you do?"

I nodded, confirming the obvious. My mind raced as I quickly made a plan. The usual strategy with this sort of thing is to pass a tube up the nostril and down into the oesophagus (the pipe that connects the mouth to the stomach), then flush it with lots of water to wash away the obstruction.

In Geronimo's case, there was too much food and it was already blocked up as far as the back of his mouth. I needed to think of another way, and fast.

"Right, Jackie," I blurted out. "Let's lift him upside down."

"What?" Jackie replied.

"I know it sounds strange, but with any luck, some of the food might fall out. He won't like it, though."

A young alpaca has a body about the size of a Labrador. Admittedly, the whole animal is much bigger – more like a small pony – but much of its size is made up of legs and neck.

Between the two of us, it would be possible to lift him and hold him upside down.

"Ready?" I said to Jackie, who nodded. "One, two, three – lift!"

As I had predicted, Geronimo did not like this plan at all and kicked and thrashed, trying to escape. The poor alpaca could hardly breathe and was panic-stricken. Holding his legs in the air and his head near the ground was another and final insult. I just hoped it would work.

I glanced to the car, where Emmy was watching with bewilderment on her little hairy face. Her head was cocked to one side, as confused as Geronimo.

What on Earth is my dad doing now? she must

have thought. *I've seen him do and say some strange things, but I've never seen him hold an alpaca upside down.*

Between us, Jackie and I massaged Geronimo's neck and reached into his mouth to pull out clumps of swollen alpaca feed. But it wasn't really working. Mushed-up food filled his throat and all the way down to his stomach. We gently lowered the little alpaca to the ground. His fluffy, limp body lay on the straw, with his long neck floppy and skinny legs pointing in all directions. He was almost lifeless. In the gloomy light of the barn, it was a sad sight. I imagined Emmy lowering her head and her ears drooping in sorrow at my failure to help poor Geronimo.

Then I had an idea – all was not lost. When lambs are born and their lungs are filled with birth fluids, vets and farmers hold them up by their back legs and swing them backwards and forwards, gently but firmly, so the fluid flies out of the mouth and nose.

"Jackie, do you think we can swing him?" I asked. "If we could, it might be possible to get some of the compacted food loose." It wasn't written down in any veterinary textbook – I was working on instinct – and Geronimo was heavy, but it was the only option left.

I took his front legs and Jackie his hind ones, then we hoisted the creature back into the air. But his neck was so long that his little head was still on the ground, so we couldn't swing him anywhere. I'd failed again.

"If we stand on that wooden food trough we might get enough height," Jackie suggested. This would require balance as well as strength and coordination, but it was worth a go.

I got up first and Jackie handed me Geronimo's front legs. I clung on with one hand before grasping the rear legs while Jackie joined me on the wooden structure. By now, surely Emmy would be covering her eyes with her paws in disbelief, but I couldn't look across to see what she thought. We had to concentrate if we were going to make this work and stand a chance at saving Geronimo.

Slowly, we started a gentle swinging motion. Eventually, we managed to coordinate our movements and Geronimo started swaying in a small arc, like the steady pendulum of an old-fashioned clock. His head was just inches from the ground and I hoped we had the strength to hold on. The last thing he needed was a bang on the head. It would be just as bad if we let go of his legs at the wrong moment. He'd fly through the air and crash in a heap.

As we desperately clung to his thin legs, Geronimo clung to his last chances of life.

All we needed was enough food to dislodge to free his throat so he could breathe. If we could make some space, then the worst part of the crisis would be over and I might be able to revert to the more conventional method, using a long plastic stomach tube and a bucket of water.

Our arms and hands ached and trembled as Geronimo was almost reaching horizontal at the top of each swing.

Please don't let go! I prayed.

Finally, and just as we were about to give in, a tennis-ball-sized matted ball of food shot from his mouth and almost hit the far wall of the barn. At the same moment, our strength gave out and we had to let go. He fell to the straw – luckily, at the low point of his swing. Then, within just a few seconds, he spluttered back to life, kicking, coughing and complaining, but very much alive!

"You've saved him!" Jackie exclaimed, relieved.

Geronimo lay in a bedraggled heap for a few moments, then lifted his head, his big black eyes wide and confused. Then, he let out a huge spluttering cough, with yet more gloopy goo exploding from his mouth and nose. I almost expected grey sludge to come out of his ears with the next cough! Geronimo looked ridiculous, but he had survived the ordeal.

"Well, not quite," I replied. "But he's certainly got a better chance now. He's definitely over the worst."

I stood back to assess the situation. Geronimo now looked more comfortable. I decided to give him a few minutes to recover from the trauma of being hoisted in the air and waved around, so I turned my attention to the other poorly alpaca. I'd hardly had a chance to examine him so far. He wasn't as bad as Geronimo, but definitely suffering from a similar obstruction.

"Could I have a bucket of warm water, please?" I asked. I would flush his obstruction through with water and a tube. If it worked, I'd move back to Geronimo, once he'd regained composure.

"This one's Apache," said Jackie, as we walked over to another young alpaca lying on the floor with his bloated stomach slowly moving up and down. "He's not as bad as Geronimo, but he's still in a poor state."

Thankfully, Apache's throat was clear, but we still need my help to empty all the extra feed in his stomach. I positioned the soft rubber tube at the entrance to Apache's nostril and slowly fed the tube down the back of his throat. Even though this feels funny, it's better than putting the tube into the mouth, because it can't be chewed by the back teeth. Once the tube wouldn't go any further, I attached a funnel to the end and then, keeping everything still, Jackie carefully poured in the water.

At one point, the flow stopped. I removed the funnel and put the end of the tube in my mouth, then sucked for all I was worth to try and unblock the tube. I knew this was risky. But finally, water flowed freely down the pipe, indicating that everything had been flushed through into the stomach. I pulled out the tube and Apache sprinted to the other side of the barn, kicking me as he passed. That was the thanks I got!

I turned back to Geronimo, to finish the job. We'd swung out the top part of the impacted food, but there was still a blockage lower down, just like the one Apache had had. When Geronimo saw me approaching with my tube, he let out a high-pitched scream. He'd just seen me insert it into his friend and didn't fancy the same treatment. And, of course, last time I'd gone towards him I'd held him in the air and swung him around.

Eventually, we had him captured and I tried to insert the pipe. But he was feeling better, stronger and more defiant, and spat, spluttered and kicked to escape. It was difficult to introduce the tube, but Jackie held on tightly. Water splattered and sprayed from the end of the stomach tube like an uncontrolled hosepipe. Soon, Jackie, Geronimo and I were all covered in the same slimy mess that was on the straw and walls of the barn.

"We're nearly there, Jackie!" I said through gritted teeth. "Just one more funnel-ful and I reckon it'll flow freely, like with Apache." It was just in time, too, because Geronimo was now completely fed up with the indignity of

the whole situation. At last, the blockage
flushed through and, with a final flourish,
he kicked and yelled some rude words in
alpaca language before jumping in the air and
running off to join his friend.

Both creatures had been saved, and while they didn't seem very pleased or grateful, Jackie certainly was. She beamed as we watched the two greedy alpacas trotting away from us. It looked like they were having a serious conversation, as far away from us as they could get.

"Did you see what they did to me?" I imagined Geronimo saying. "Upside down! Then they waved me around like a child's swing! What a disgrace!"

"And they pushed a pipe up my nose!" Apache might have said.

It had been a very unusual and challenging morning. Both Jackie and I were tired and hungry but immensely satisfied. Between us, we'd saved two lives, one in a very unconventional fashion!

After a clean-up and a welcome cup of coffee at Jackie's house, I rejoined Emmy in the car. Once the initial excitement of seeing me hold a woolly alpaca upside down had gone, she'd clearly lost interest in our antics and I found her curled up asleep on my seat.

"Up you get, Em. We need to go now."

She moved reluctantly but sensed things might soon become more interesting.

"That was pretty hairy!" I said. "And I don't mean the alpaca. I thought we were going to lose Geronimo for a moment," I confided, now feeling the exertion of the morning's activities catching up on me.

By now it was daylight and the mist was slowly lifting. Emmy needed a walk, and we would be passing one of her favourite spots on the way back. At the bend in the road there was a lay-by with a path that led to the top of a little hill. Emmy knew it well and started to get excited at the prospect of a run across the fields covered in a blanket of frost.

I opened the door and with her typical pent-up energy she leapt upwards and outwards onto the path, landing several metres away on the muddy grass. As my energetic little dog flew through the air, I couldn't help myself from shouting at the top of my voice, "GERONIMO!" It was a good job there was nobody about to hear me!

Lambing Time

Hagg Farm was on top of a small hill and the long drive up the lane was always a pleasant experience. It was a quiet road, totally free of other traffic. On a busy afternoon, you might encounter a horse with rider or possibly a couple of walkers. Maybe a rabbit or a field mouse scurrying across the track.

I knew the lane like the back of my hand –

a gentle bend to the left, then a long straight and flat bit, just before the tight right-hand corner, then another left before the steady climb up to the farmhouse. On a misty morning, the farm was high enough to sit above the low-lying mist. It had views across the valley and over to the bigger hills in the far distance.

On this particular evening, the roads and nearby fields were the territory of owls, foxes and badgers. Not to mention the frosty

hedgerows that glittered in the moonlight as I rounded a corner. Emmy was also enjoying the ride and made excited noises as we continued on in the dark. She loved watching out for wildlife as much as I did.

Even when it was a dark and cold night or during a busy day, I loved a visit to Hagg Farm, and tonight I was happy in the knowledge that I'd be delivering a lamb or two, as it was lambing time at the farm. While many lambs are born during the spring months, the sheep at Hagg Farm started having their lambs before Christmas through to late February.

The Peckitt brothers were very appreciative of the work their vets did for them during this time. Some farmers tried to avoid calling us out, because of the extra expense, but the Peckitts were always pleased to see me.

This evening's call was like many others I'd had recently. I'd just got in from work and it was my turn to be on duty again. I hadn't even had a chance to make a cup of tea before the phone rang.

"Julian, we need some help with the sheep again," came John Peckitt's voice down the line.

"I'm on my way," I replied cheerily.

Ten minutes later, I was nearing the end of my journey, eager to get to the farm. I had been a regular visitor to Hagg Farm at this special time of year, when new lambs appeared like rabbits from a magician's hat. There was little chance to rest or recover, as I was constantly busy, but with new life everywhere, it was definitely magical.

The Peckitts were superb shepherds – extremely hard-working and dedicated, and totally devoted to their sheep.

Their only problem – and one that was impossible to resolve – was that both brothers had HUGE hands.

Huge hands were an advantage for shovelling things, carrying heavy bales of hay or moving stubborn sheep from one place to another, but a terrible disadvantage when it came to assisting a ewe that was struggling to give birth. Their hands were simply too big for the delicate operation of untangling a lamb.

The result of the brothers' huge-hand situation was that they had to call out the vet to deal with nearly every sheep that needed even the slightest bit of help. They once had to call the practice FIVE times in a single day, which is still a record!

My car skidded a little as I rounded the last bend into the farm. I'd have to be careful on this icy night. But as I focused on the

challenge ahead of me and the prospect
of half an hour or so chatting with my old
farmer friends, I soon forgot about the
icy roads. Before long, we had arrived.
I turned off the ignition and patted Emmy
on the head.

"Crikey, that last corner was a bit slippery,"
I muttered. She looked up, apparently totally
unaware of the icy roads, her dark eyes full
of trust. "You'll have to stay put for this one,
Em. We don't want to spook the sheep."
Emmy settled back down in her spot on the
passenger seat. I wondered if she was relieved
that she didn't have to venture out into the
chilly farm.

"Hello," John said cheerily as I climbed
out of the car and pulled on my wellies and
waterproof trousers. He was a large man with
a round red face. His brother, Tom, who was
smaller in all ways (apart from his hands

of course) was standing next to John, as he usually did.

"It's a gimmer and she's been on for a while. We thought we'd better call the expert," Tom said.

A gimmer is a young sheep who is having her first lamb. They usually have more problems having their lambs because the space is often restricted and delivery can take longer. I reckoned vets at my practice had probably delivered every lamb from every gimmer at Hagg Farm, so it was no surprise to any of us that I'd been called to help this evening.

The brothers and I approached the barn, and the young sheep was easy to spot, lying flat on her side. This is not a normal comfortable position for a sheep, so I knew she must be in trouble. She strained and extended her head and neck, pulling a funny

face each time she pushed, her eyes bulging
with the effort. I immediately felt sorry for
her, as I'd seen plenty of sheep like this.

"There, there," I said and gave her a rub on
her fleecy back to offer some comfort.

As a first-time mum, the young ewe didn't know what to expect – it was all new to her. It was a painful and confusing experience, so before I offered my assistance, what I really wanted to do was reassure her.

"Everything will be all right," I said gently. "Don't worry, I'm here." The ewe let out a little bleat. I turned back to Tom.

"Any idea of how big the lamb is?" I asked.

"It's a fair size," Tom said. He'd tried to deliver the lamb before calling me, so he knew how big it was.

"I'll have a feel and see what I can make of it," I said, plunging my right hand into the bucket of water that had already been prepared. On this cold night, steam billowed from the bucket like smoke from a dragon's nostrils. I was relieved the water was warm!

Next, I applied a generous blob of gel to my palm and rubbed it up my arms, then made my first cautious and gentle exploration, hoping that my light manipulations would quickly provide relief from her discomfort.

This is always the most exciting part, because it's the first time I can get a sense of what is in store for me. Would there be more than one lamb? Maybe it was just one big single lamb, trying to squeeze through a small space? Now was the moment when I'd be able to work it out and come up with a plan.

The ewe let out a surprised bleat and her eyes bulged even more, but she quickly settled. I hoped she could tell I was there to help her.

"It's a big single 'un, I'll bet," John shouted, anticipating what I might be about to say. "And I'm not sure it'll come out that way!" he added with confidence, pessimistic about my chances.

"Let 'im get on wi' it, our lad! He knows what he's doin'!" Tom cut in, gently chastising his bigger brother. He had more confidence in my chances of a successful delivery. "And he's got nice small hands!"

But immediately I was worried. As predicted by John, the lamb was large. To make matters worse, its head was bent forwards with the nose pointing downwards, as if bowing its head. That was all I could feel so far, so my first step was to reposition the head so its nose was pointing towards the way out. With the benefit of my "nice small hands", I could just about slip a finger under the lamb's chin and flip up the nose.

"I've got its head lined up now, but the next problem is that I can't find any legs," I explained to the onlookers. "The trouble is, there's not enough space for head and legs to come together."

"I knew it," said John triumphantly. "It's too big for a young sheep like that. It's sure to be a single and it'll never come out that way. There's only one way now!"

We all knew what the other way was. The poor ewe might need to have surgery to get the lamb out. In experienced hands, the surgery usually goes very well, but operating in the darkness of a dirty barn can be fraught with problems. It is far removed from a clean and sterile operating theatre, so it's always better if the lambs can be delivered by the natural route if possible. It's a big decision and most farmers and vets would regard it as a last resort.

I edged my fingers further in, until I could just touch two feet. I needed to extend them both so that the chin rested on the stretched-out legs to have any chance of getting the lamb out. Was John right? Should I be

reaching for my surgical kit? *Not just yet,*
I thought and wriggled my fingers still
further until I could just reach one foot.
Grasping it between two fingers, like you
might hold a pair of chopsticks, I pulled.
Finally, the foot extended and I had the head
and one foot in the right position. The foot
was visible now and Tom was quick to make
the first comment.

"You see, our lad, he's already got a leg.
I told you he could do it!"

"I've still got some work to do, Tom. The
next bit is the hardest," I said. Now I needed
to position the second leg. I could touch it, but
each time I extended my fingers far enough,
Mum would push and strain, trapping my
fingers. I tried not to complain, but I knew
my face was developing similar distorted
expressions to those of the soon-to-be mother.
My own eyes were beginning to bulge too.

Between the ewe's pushes, I tried the same technique as before, but it was hard and I was soon huffing and puffing as much as the ewe, with searing pain in my fingers.

"If I can just reach that foot," I said between gasps.

I managed to get a firm hold and repeated the same process until, at last, the second leg was where I wanted it.

"Got it!" I rejoiced.

"I told you, John. He's a good lamber is Julian. I knew he'd do it," said Tom.

"Hang on a minute," I protested. "It's not out yet! This is just stage one complete. Head and legs are lined up, but it's still going to be a squeeze. There's no guarantee this lamb will fit. As John says, it's a big 'un."

Now it was time for my lambing ropes. Looping them around each foot made it easier to pull. Without them, tired hands quickly slipped away from the legs. I fished around for them in the bottom of the bucket, the water now tepid rather than hot. Blue for left, red for right was my usual pattern and, once they were in place, I started to pull gently. Slowly, the legs and nose started to emerge. Surely it wouldn't be this easy? Would the lamb drop onto the straw in just a few seconds?

The answer to both questions was no – it wasn't and it didn't. The rest of the head refused to follow and progress ground to a halt.

John was quick to interject with more advice. "Is it stuck? If you need to do an operation, you'd better do it now before it gets jammed proper."

My plastic bottle of lubricant had a long nozzle, which made it possible to squirt extra gel into tight places. I reached for my bottle and squirted a large blob of gel behind the lamb's head, which made a funny noise. Then the ewe made a similar funny noise as she let out a loud gurgling sound before a lamb landed with a gentle thud on the straw.

John and Tom were next to emit loud noises – they both whooped with delight and congratulations, patting each other and me on the back.

"Told yer!" said Tom.

Meanwhile, as Mum recovered her strength for a moment or two, the lamb lifted its head and flapped its ears, unaware of the massive effort required by both his mother and me to bring him into the cold and frosty world.

"Job's a good 'un," said John, which from him was praise indeed.

I stood back and gazed at the lamb for a few moments. This was the best bit of my job.

New life always seems a miracle and being part of that miracle is a privilege and a thrill that never fades. Watching a new lamb find its feet and bond with its mother as she licks it all over is brilliant.

Everyone was pleased with a good evening's work. All I needed now was a clean-up. Tom produced another bucket of hot water to wash my arms and rinse my leggings and wellies (as usual, I'd made a big mess), then I was ready to head home.

"Well, that's me finished for tonight,"
I said. "I'm off for a well-deserved cup of tea."

"I expect so!" Tom laughed. "We'll be in touch, no doubt."

The night sky was still clear and the moon bright as I cruised down the farm lane, full of happy feelings. Emmy scanned the hedgerows, hoping to see an owl swooping off on its night's hunting.

"Nearly there, Em," I said. I was tired and ready for bed.

But as the bend approached, something wasn't right. I turned my steering wheel to drive round it, as I usually did, but the car didn't respond. Instead of rounding the bend, I slid forwards, slowly but totally out of control, then veered off the smooth surface of the lane.

Bump, bump, bang, crash and then silence.
I was in the hedge.

"Bother!" I said loudly, holding my head in my hands. Emmy jumped up in a start. Luckily, she hadn't been hurt, but I stroked her to calm her down. "You idiot, Julian," I told myself.

I sat there for a few moments, trying to work out what to do. I was in the middle of the dark Yorkshire countryside, stuck in a hedge. I quickly realized the first thing was to get out of the car, which was easier said than done, because tangled and broken branches seemed to be wrapped around the doors and windscreen. I tried the driver's side door, which was jammed shut, then the passenger door – also stuck.

Dishevelled, I finally squeezed out of a back door, with Emmy jumping out of the car behind me. The poor dog must have been shocked and concerned, but as long as she was with me, everything would be OK.

We stood and surveyed the moonlit scene of destruction. It didn't look good. Both front wheels were embedded in the hedge and the back wheels rested clumsily on the grassy verge.

I'll have to walk up to the farmhouse and get some assistance, I thought. *Maybe a tractor could help?*

Emmy cocked her head as if to say, "I don't know… I don't drive."

"Come on then, Em. Back to Hagg Farm we go!"

I trudged back up the hill to the farm, Emmy on her lead. We were an embarrassed and miserable sight as I knocked on the farmhouse door. Tom answered it.

"Well, I'm happy to see you, Julian, but this was sooner than we meant!" He laughed.

"I'm really sorry. I've skidded on the ice and my car is stuck in your hedge," I said, turning and pointing down the hill. "Any chance of a tow from a tractor?"

"You're not the first person to do that, so don't you worry about it," Tom said with a grin. "I'll get the tractor. We'll pull you out in no time. John, give us a hand to pull vet'nary out of the 'edge! He's gone straight on down at bottom o' lane!"

We chugged slowly back down in the tractor, Tom driving, with Emmy happily sat on his lap, her ears blowing in the icy breeze. John was next to them and I was perched on the footplate, half out of the door. Clinging to a metal handle, my hands were freezing, but I was grateful for the help. For once, it was me asking them for assistance.

I jumped off the tractor when we arrived at the accident zone. The moon was still silvery white, but the huge lights on the front of the tractor lit up the scene like a theatre stage.

I stood back to leave John and Tom to organize everything. Farmers are very skilled at manoeuvring tractors to pull things, and vets are not. I was no help with this job.

Tom aligned the tractor and John arranged the chain, but soon stopped and shook his head slowly from side to side. Then he said, for the second time that evening, "D'you know what? I'm not sure it'll come out that way!"

"Well, we've been proven wrong before!" Tom laughed.

The brothers' tractor heaved and strained and it pulled with all its power until eventually the car came free from the hedge. Emmy barked to thank them as they guided the car down from the verge. It had been quite a night. We were all tired and cold, but I couldn't wait for the next call to come and visit Hagg Farm. I just hoped that it would be a little less eventful!

Catching Kittens

After my car accident on the ice, Emmy and I were confined to the practice while my car was at the garage being patched up. So, it was small-animal-only duties for me for the time being. This was fine, because I love treating dogs and cats, rabbits, guinea pigs and ferrets as well as chatting to their owners.

Mixed practice work is great, because there is almost endless variety. Every day is different. And, for a few days at least, I wouldn't be exposed to the harsh and bitter cold of a Yorkshire winter. I could guarantee warm hands, snug feet and no stress or major traumas. Or so I thought…

"I've only managed to catch two of them, I'm afraid," said Mr Gill, almost apologetically as he stepped into my consulting room.

He was carrying a rusty old cat cage, which was covered in cobwebs and leaves. I wondered what kind of animals he had inside. The cage was quite small, so they must be little. I peered in and could see a sloping platform, on which food could be placed to tempt a hungry animal inside. When it stood on the platform, the door suddenly fell, capturing it in the cage.

Old-fashioned as the contraption looked, it was the only way to manage an appointment with a small wild animal and a vet.

Inside, two kittens, wide-eyed and spiky with fear, huddled and hissed from the back corner of the container. One was ginger and the other was grey. They both had blue eyes and were very cute. But both, I felt sure, would be wild and difficult to handle.

"They must be about four or five months old by now," the old man explained. "Their mum appeared with them back in September. By gum, they were small then, nowt but balls of fluff. Are they big enough to neuter? I hope so, 'cos that's what I've fetched 'em in for."

It was difficult to tell how big they were, partly because they were sitting on top of each other and partly because a frightened cat makes its fur stand on end, in an attempt to look bigger and ward off would-be attackers. These two kittens hadn't seen many humans before, let alone been captured in a wire trap, then put on a table for a strange man to stare at. They were, quite naturally, worried. In reality, their spiked-up fur just made the kittens look fluffier and not at all intimidating – to me, they just looked really cute.

I did some quick maths. If they had arrived at Mr Gill's farm in September, they should be almost five months old now. They were certainly still kittens, but I could tell they were not friendly at all but wild, unhandled, frightened animals. The best thing we could do was check them over and then neuter them, which would help them become a little calmer and more friendly.

"I think they'll be OK to do now, Mr Gill," I confirmed. "You've done well to catch them and we should take the chance to sort them out."

"There's plenty more on the farm," he added. "One day there were two kittens. The next day there were five. The next day there were seven. And by the next day there were nine of 'em. The mum kept bringing 'em two or three at a time. She must've thought that my farm was a safe place for 'em to grow up.

They made a lovely snug home in the hay barn. But they're as wick as eels. You can't touch 'em. They run off like lightning into the hay bales. It'll take me a week or more to get them all captured, I think. I need to gain their trust," he said, placing special emphasis on the word "trust".

"It must be a nice life, living on your farm," I said. "They'll keep the mice down, and I bet, in return, they get a drop of milk that's left over from the cows?"

I knew Mr Gill quite well, because he had a small dairy herd and I'd been treating his cows. The last time I'd seen him was on a sunny day in the autumn. A cow had gone down with a serious infection. She was lying in the middle of a giant thorny gorse bush on the sun-drenched slopes of a field and was too poorly to stand up. We'd both got thoroughly prickled as we treated her on the hillside.

"It should be an easier job for you today," he said with a chuckle.

I looked at the tiny young cats in the cage. They were a thousand times smaller than the cow in the bush, but I knew they'd present a challenge that was just as large. Wild cats are hard to handle and uncooperative in equal measure. They have sharp and spiky claws on each paw and pointy teeth, which they're not afraid to use.

"Leave them with me and I'll get them sorted for you," I said confidently. "They'll be good to go home by the middle of the afternoon." I took the basket into the small cat-kennel area, where it was quiet and safe, away from scary dogs. Handling the critters would be the hardest part of checking them over. But I'd done this many times before. I needed to be quick and efficient. *What could possibly go wrong?* I told myself.

We use a special injection for cats like these to make them a bit sleepy, so that they're easier to handle. It just needs to be injected somewhere you can reach without getting scratched or bitten. After ten minutes, if the dose is calculated correctly, the cat is asleep for about forty-five minutes – ample time to do the checks I needed to do and carry out the procedure.

I drew up the initial dose and prepared to inject the first patient. If I could poke my syringe and needle through one of the gaps in the wire cage, I'd be able to inject each kitten. My plan was simple, but not guaranteed to work. Often cats don't like this and spin round in response to the needle, as if suddenly stung by a bee.

But I was lucky. The ginger kitten was sitting right at the side of the basket and surprisingly didn't react to the injection.

I managed to press the plunger and inject the full dose in one motion. Feeling smug, I settled back to drink my coffee while I waited for kitten number one to drift off to sleep.

I had only got halfway through my coffee by the time the little ginger fluff ball was sleeping soundly. I reached into the cage to grasp the dozing kitten, taking care to open the door only enough to squeeze my hand inside. I didn't want its friend to escape, or scratch or bite me either, but it lurked warily at the back of the cage. Obviously, it was even more anxious and confused than it had been when they arrived. *Why has my friend suddenly fallen asleep when we are in this predicament?* the grey kitten must have been thinking.

Ginger, as we'd named it, turned out to be a boy, so he needed a quick and simple procedure to be neutered. It all went smoothly and I prepared to pop the drowsy

kitten back into the basket with Grey. This is where it all went wrong. As I slid Ginger back into the basket, Grey seized the opportunity to make a bid for freedom.

Grey definitely did not want to meet the same fate as Ginger and burst out of the semi-open door. Suddenly, loose in the small cat-kennel area, the kitten developed superpowers and ran, leapt and levitated with such force that it burst through the polystyrene ceiling tiles and disappeared, leaving just the tilted tile through which it had vanished.

The cheeky cat had escaped into the roof space above. I couldn't believe what had just happened. My mouth was still wide open in horror when Natasha the nurse appeared, having heard the commotion in the kennels.

"The little grey cat has escaped! It's gone up there," I said, pointing upwards to the small gap in the tiles. I was devastated.

"What? It's gone into the roof?" Natasha asked, astonished.

"It's gone into the roof," I repeated, feeling foolish. I was still stunned. How was this even possible? I rechecked the cat container. Had I imagined it? But the wire cage was completely empty. There was no doubt the pesky kitten had scaled the whole height of the smooth and shiny kennel wall, and disappeared into the attic.

"I've never seen that happen before." I said, still incredulous at Grey's speed and power. "It was moving quickly and completely vertically. We'd better get a stepladder and a torch."

I put Ginger into another basket, so that he could recover peacefully, then headed to investigate the roof space with my torch. The roof space was made of polystyrene tiles, suspended by metal wires, so it would be impossible to climb in. So, I used the ladder to clamber on top of the kennel unit, then lifted another of the ceiling tiles and peered into the void.

I expected to see the kitten sitting right in front of me, just as surprised at its superpowers as I was. But the acrobatic cat was nowhere to be seen. This left us with a big problem. The whole area seemed to be sealed, so there was no chance the kitten could have escaped outside.

On closer investigation, in the very furthest corner, one wide pipe with an open end led downwards. Was Grey at the bottom of it? Should I lower a rope down to try and hoist him out? It was all too confusing and stressful to make a simple decision.

Vets and nurses had a hurried meeting about the disastrous situation with Grey.

The plan we came up with was to place the cage in the roof, with its wire trap full of tasty food and tempting treats for a hungry kitten. Hopefully it would simply walk into the cage when it needed food or water. This had worked before, back in Mr Gill's hay barn, so I hoped it would work again. Unless, of course, it had found a way out – or was stranded down the pipe.

With a heavy heart, I picked up the phone to call Mr Gill.

"Hi, Mr Gill," I said quietly. "The ginger kitten is fine, recovering nicely. He's a boy, by the way. But there's a problem with the little grey cat."

I explained what had happened, fearing a tirade of anger because I'd lost Mr Gill's kitten. I described the forceful energy with which it had burst through the lightweight roof tile and how this had never happened to me before. I also explained our optimistic plan to recapture the kitten.

"Ah, try not to worry. These things happen. I'm sure the little rascal will turn up before too long. It's always first at the food and milk, so I expect it'll be tempted down by breakfast," came the reply. I breathed a cautious sigh of relief. While I was very worried about the cat, at least I wasn't also facing the wrath of an annoyed owner.

Mr Gill collected Ginger later that day, but Grey was still in hiding. Every half an hour or so, someone would poke their head into the dark roof space, holding a torch, to look for lost Grey and check the cage. And every time, they would return looking glum. There was no cat to be seen.

At the end of the day, I switched off the lights in the practice and got ready to head home. Emmy was waiting for me by the front door. She wagged her tail as I walked towards her, but not even her happiness to see me could lift my spirits. I felt awful that I'd lost the kitten, and now the poor frightened little creature would be even more anxious in the dark and silence of the roof above the practice. It was a long way from the warm, cosy comfort of a hay barn. Everyone hoped the morning would bring success and that we would find Grey sitting, with a full belly, inside the cat trap.

Emmy and I arrived very early the next morning to a gloomy welcome. Grey was either still on the loose, hiding in a dark corner, or stuck at the bottom of the ominous and wide open-ended pipe. Everyone tried to get on with their normal work, but no matter how many animals we attended to, we couldn't help but feel distracted by the cat-in-the-roof situation.

An elderly Labrador called Leo was first on my list. He was struggling with sore and stiff hips as a result of arthritis and was finding it increasingly difficult and painful to get around. Liz, his owner, recalled some amusing stories from his younger years as I examined him.

"He was a real character when he was a puppy," she explained with tears welling up in her eyes. "He learnt how to open doors, so he kept escaping and getting into places he shouldn't!"

My heart lurched again. An escaping dog! *That doesn't sound very funny*, I thought to myself, immediately reminded of poor Grey.

"Then, he learnt how to open jars as well," Liz went on. "One day, I came home from work and Leo had opened the kitchen door, then opened a jar of marmalade and he'd EATEN IT ALL!" She laughed, adding, "And I was really cross because I was looking forward to some

crusty bread and marmalade but there was
none left. He's been such an amazing dog.
I hope you can help him."

I fussed Leo, rubbing his fuzzy ears,
imagining him licking up a whole jar of
marmalade. "I'm sure we can, Liz, so please
don't worry." I arranged some medication to
help with Leo's arthritis. "This should help
him," I added as I handed over the tablets.
"Better than marmalade, anyway!"

Lunchtime arrived. Each check of the trap and roof had been unsuccessful. The lost grey kitten was causing increasing concern and anxiety for everyone. We took it in turns to poke our heads through the lifted polystyrene tiles to peer into the darkness, looking for signs of life. There was never any noise or the smallest clue that little Grey was there. But where could it have gone?

I decided to fetch a rope and try to get close to the wide pipe, where I suspected Grey might be trapped. I'd lower the end down and the stricken kitten might be able to use the rope to climb out. I could tie knots every so often to make it easier for Grey to climb up. Everyone agreed it was not a plan with high chances of success, but we were running out of options.

I was just getting my coat on, ready to go and rummage in my garage at home for an appropriate rope, when shrieks came from the kennel. Natasha soon appeared, a smile beaming across her face, with Emmy trotting in happily beside her.

"Look who Emmy found!" she exclaimed, clutching the metal cage with a very embarrassed-looking grey cat sitting in the middle, a few cobwebs clinging to its dusty fur. "She must have heard the kitten scratching about and came to find me."

"Good girl, Emmy!" we all cried. "You've saved the day!" Emmy twirled around excitedly as the nurses made a huge fuss of her.

I looked inside the cage. "Where have you been hiding?" I said to little Grey. "You've had us all very worried!"

Of course, Grey didn't reply. Relieved beyond measure, I made a call to Mr Gill with the good news.

"We'd better get this little one sorted,"
I suggested. "Then the sooner we get it back
to the hay barn the better, I think."

This time, we took no chances and Grey
put up no objection to the injection.

I examined the snoozing kitten.
"Grey, you're a girl!" I exclaimed. But she
couldn't hear me. She was fast asleep,
dreaming, I suspected, about her exciting
game of hide-and-seek in the roof.

As I looked at Grey's tiny face, I couldn't help but wonder how many more exciting adventures she would have on Mr Gill's farm with all the other animals.

Man's Best Friend

Mr Bellerby's old dog, Bess, hadn't been quite right for a couple of weeks, so he had brought her in for another check-up. I had a bad feeling that Bess might be very poorly and my heart sank as the laboratory machine chugged out the paper slip showing her latest test results. All the important readings were off the scale.

I stepped out of the room and took a moment to think. Explaining bad news to a doting owner is always awful. I know first-hand how much a dog means to an owner. As if she had read my thoughts, Emmy suddenly appeared in the corridor and tilted her head inquisitively. I gave her a stroke and a quick hug before I returned to the consulting room, where Bess and Mr Bellerby were waiting anxiously.

I gave Bess a fuss around her ears and scratched under her chin. Her head rested wearily on my hand, but her tail thumped a couple of times in response. She knew I was trying to help but her eyes had lost the shine that was once there. Only a few months before, I had been to Mr Bellerby's farm to treat a sheep. Bess had been a whirling dervish of sleek black-and-white energy as she'd charged around the hills, rounding up the flock at high speed. Then, she had been lively and vigorous, but not today.

I explained the situation to Mr Bellerby, then added, "We can try an intravenous drip to give her some medicine, which should make her feel a bit better for a while. But I'm afraid that she's very poorly."

"I understand," said Mr Bellerby, with tears welling in his eyes. "I think I'll take her home for a few days. Feed her sausages and take her to all her special places – down to the woods and maybe on the moors if she'll make it that far. And give her one last time with the sheep, if she wants. And then I'll call you when the time is right. If she can make it to Christmas, that'll be nice."

I nodded in agreement. This was the best and most fitting plan, and it would give Bess and Mr Bellerby the chance to spend a little more time together. But secretly, I knew that getting to Christmas was unlikely. Poor Bess was seriously ill and I didn't think she had long left.

It was only two days later when Mr Bellerby phoned back and asked me to go up to his farm to see Bess. Emmy hopped in the car beside me, blissfully unaware of the difficult morning that awaited me at the farm.

"Come in," Mr Bellerby said, opening the heavy farmhouse door before I'd even had a chance to knock. "You'll have to just ignore me. I'm gonna be an awful mess," he continued, tears already spilling down his pale face. "She's been a great old friend and I'm gonna miss her terribly."

I held back my tears as best I could as I thought about my own best friend, Emmy, waiting for me back in the car. But now was the time to help Bess, and I resolved

myself to do my very best and make her as comfortable as I could.

Bess was lying on the sofa, snuggled up in a pile of thick blankets. It seemed a strange place for a farm dog who had spent most of her life outside and on the hills. She looked cosy, despite being weak.

"She's been in here ever since she's been poorly," Mr Bellerby admitted. "I couldn't bear to leave her in the kennel. She's right enjoyed the fuss. But I know that it's time for us to say goodbye. Will you help her on her way?"

I nodded in agreement and reassured Mr Bellerby. He was right. The kindest thing to do would be to give Bess an injection that would help her drift off into a last deep sleep. I got my equipment ready and gave Bess a soothing stroke on her fur. Mr Bellerby and I had enjoyed plenty of happy times, lambing sheep and treating calves, but none of them could make up for the sadness of today. I try to be compassionate and caring but efficient and careful. Today, as the injection trickled in and Bess peacefully closed her eyes, I was all these things, but inside I was crying, just like Mr Bellerby, her lifelong friend.

Afterwards, I took the long way back to the practice. I was in no rush to chat to colleagues about my morning visit and wanted to take in the views over the Dales. I pulled off the road at the top of a hill and walked a short distance from the car. Emmy rushed around as usual, excited to be out for a new adventure, however brief it might be.

The Dales were just as beautiful as always, expansive and calming. The winter sun was weak and low in the sky. Mist lingered in the hollows and on this quiet and windless day, smoke rose vertically from the chimneys of houses scattered along the valley bottom. It was a view I knew well, though it was different every time. The light changed through the day and the shades of fields changed through the seasons – greens, browns, yellows and even purples on the far tops of the moors in summer. And they stretched on, almost for ever.

I looked down on this landscape and thought about all of the wonderful times Bess must have had on these very fields. Then I thought of all the animals I'd treated and all those under my care, of various types

and sizes – all creatures great and small.
After today, there was one fewer patient for
me to look after, but that was how it had to
be. Whatever happens, however sad, there
are always animals that need help.

"Come on then," I said to Emmy. She
trotted alongside me obediently as I picked
myself up and got back to work.

"Look what someone has just brought
in!" exclaimed Fiona the nurse as I walked
in through the back door of the practice.
In her arms was the fluffiest puppy I'd ever
seen. Immediately, vets and nurses appeared
from every part of the practice, their work
abandoned. When a cute puppy is in the
building, everyone comes running.

Fiona explained what had happened as the
puppy sat stock-still in her arms, one huge
ear cocked up and the other hanging down,
looking anxious.

"He was found by the side of the road.
The poor thing must've been terrified!"
she told the assembled crowd. "I said we'd
get a vet to check him over, see if he's got a
microchip and keep him here while we try to
find an owner. He might be lost. Though I
can't imagine how anyone would let him out
of their sight. He's gorgeous!"

I volunteered immediately. After my morning, I needed a happy moment and checking over a puppy is one of the best things about my job. They are always cute and interested in everything. It's great fun listening to their heart and breathing with a stethoscope, and checking their eyes, ears and teeth while avoiding most of the licks.

Fiona reluctantly released the pup from her cuddle and placed him on the table of my consulting room. He had bright blue eyes and wonky ears, one drooping forwards and down, and the other sticking upwards and backwards. He had a thick, woolly coat, which made it difficult to work out how big or small he really was, and he had the markings of a wolf. Nobody could tell what type of dog he was going to be!

"Hello, little one," I said, gently starting to check him over. "Let's have a look at you."

My examination was thorough but punctuated by cuddles. The poor little thing was a healthy boy, but he was worried and confused.

The final part of the health check and cuddling involved checking for a microchip. These are tiny pellets, about as big as a grain of rice, which are implanted in dogs, cats, horses and sometimes tortoises. They transmit a number, which is registered to the animal's owner on a database. When an animal is found and brought into the vet's, we scan it with a microchip scanner in the hope of finding a fifteen-digit number that will link it back to its owner.

It can be a moment of great joy. Once, when we found a stray cat, we checked it for a microchip and a number appeared on the little screen. We contacted the database company and they gave us an address that was many miles from where the cat had been found. What on Earth could have happened?

When we called the telephone number we'd been given, the lady couldn't believe her ears. A small miracle had occurred. "I assumed I'd never see him again," she cried tearfully down the phone as we relayed the happy news. "We thought he'd climbed onto the milkman's float and been taken away by accident. He's been gone for about four years!"

So today I waved the scanner over the ball of fluff and closed my eyes, waiting for the beep. There was silence. I opened my eyes and tried again. Maybe the batteries were low? Still no beep, no number, no owner. We all knew this meant the puppy had been abandoned rather than lost.

Fiona immediately scooped him up, clearly struggling to believe that someone could have abandoned this beautiful soft pup. "We'll have to keep him here for a few days, in case there is an owner somewhere. Perhaps they haven't had the chance to get him chipped. In the meantime, little man, we need to think of a name for you!"

For the rest of the day, the nurses took turns to carry the nameless pup around, and when work in the practice became too busy, he was put in a kennel for food and sleep. As it neared the time for everyone to go home, there had still been no contact from anyone looking for a missing puppy, so Fiona took him home that night, to make sure he was well looked after.

The next day, the puppy was back. We decided he should be called "Gus" because it sounded like "fuss", which is what we were all making of the little fuzzy puppy. As time went on, Gus became more confident around people and even started to wag his tail. He was enjoying his stay at the practice, and all the vets and nurses loved him. The problem was, we all knew he couldn't stay for ever.

One afternoon, Mr Bellerby called in to collect some bottles of medicine for his sheep. Soon lambing time would start on his farm and he wanted to stock up on supplies for the busiest time of his year. As he reached the bottom of his list and carefully packed the last few items in his cardboard box, I heard him say to Sylvia, the receptionist, "Is Julian in? Can I have a word?"

I wandered through to reception to have a chat with Mr Bellerby.

"Thank you for what you did for Bess," he said quietly. "It was a hard decision, but it was for the best. Thank you for being so kind and I'm sorry for being such a wreck. It hit me hard."

"It's OK, Mr Bellerby," I said.

We chatted for a while about Bess and all the happy times Mr Bellerby had shared with her, then about the lambing time to come. Just like at Hagg Farm, Mr Bellerby had a type of sheep that always started lambing around Christmas, much earlier than some of the moorland or hill sheep, which always lambed when spring and warmer weather were on their way.

Before long, Fiona appeared, clutching the final bottle of medicine from Mr Bellerby's list in one hand and Gus tucked under her other arm.

"Hi, Mr Bellerby," she said. "I'm so sorry to hear about Bess."

"Oh, thank you," Mr Bellerby replied in a low voice.

"Here's the bottle of calcium you needed. Oh, and this is Gus." Fiona told him the story of Gus and the circumstances of his arrival at the practice, before adding, "And he's looking for a new home."

Mr Bellerby's eyes widened and a smile grew across his face. I guessed it was the first time he'd smiled in many weeks. It was at that moment that I had an idea.

"A pup like Gus would fit in nicely on your farm, Mr Bellerby," I ventured. "He's not a Border collie, I'm pretty sure of that, but he's a lovely pup. He'd be a great friend, even if he doesn't know how to work with sheep."

"Maybe," Mr Bellerby replied, without committing himself. He picked up the box of medication and headed out of the door. But only a few moments later he returned.

"So, he's looking for a new home is he, this pup you've got?"

"He is," I replied.

"And he's definitely got no owner?"

"Not that we can find," I said. "And much as we'd love to, we can't keep him here."

"Can I hold of 'im'?" Mr Bellerby asked.

"Of course!" I smiled as Fiona handed Gus over. The little pup snuggled into Mr Bellerby's shoulder, then licked him on his face affectionately.

Mr Bellerby couldn't help but laugh as Gus said hello to him in his own special way. "I think Gus would be reet suited to a life on my farm. If it's OK with everyone 'ere, I'd like to have 'im."

It didn't take long before Gus was strapped into the front seat of Mr Bellerby's car, ready to go. Vets and nurses lined up to see them off. There were lots of smiles and just a few tears. We were sad to see him go, but Gus would have a lovely life on the farm and Mr Bellerby, beaming broadly, was the happiest farmer I'd seen all week.

"I'll catch up next time I'm out to a lambing," I said, feeling in a small way triumphant that both Gus's life and Mr Bellerby's were about to be transformed.

"That'll be nice, but I hope I don't need to call you out too much over Christmas," Mr Bellerby replied with a nod. "And thank you for this pup. He's cheered me up no end."

As December progressed, I was desperate for a visit to Mr Bellerby's farm. I couldn't wait to see how Gus was settling into life on the farm. And I didn't have to wait too long. I'd nearly finished my morning round of calls when my phone rang. It was Sylvia, the receptionist at the practice.

"Hi, Julian. Can you go to Mr Bellerby's? He has a lamb with a sore eye."

"Of course," I replied. "I'm just finishing here so I'll head out soon."

The call I was on was straightforward. I was back at Castle Farm, checking up on a cow after another tricky delivery. Once I'd finished, Mr Towton showed me Duchess and her calf. I was pleased to see that both were doing well and thriving.

I said my goodbyes and headed off to Mr Bellerby's farm, which wasn't far from

Castle Farm, so it wasn't long before I was driving into his yard.

"Hello again," called Mr Bellerby as he strode out to meet me. "I have a newborn lamb with a sore eye. I think it needs one of those injections you give to sort it out."

Mr Bellerby was referring to a common condition where the eyelid rolls inwards and rubs on the surface of the eye, making it sore. And he was right. It's simple to fix with an injection that quickly corrects the problem.

"I'd have fetched it down to the practice, but I wanted you to come and have a look at this little pup," he added. "I thought you'd like to see how he's settling in."

As I prepared the injection that I'd need for the lamb, a chaotic whirl of fluff raced towards me. At very high speed, Gus came rushing around the corner. His tail was wagging enthusiastically and his face looked

like he was grinning. I bent down to my
knees on the drive to say hello.

"Hi, Gus! How are you? Do you remember
me? How's life on the farm?"

But this was clearly too many questions
for little Gus. He jumped up and licked me
all over, paying particular attention to my
hands, on which still clung the vague aroma
from the cow I'd been treating at Castle Farm.

I hoped he recognized me, but even if not, it didn't matter. Gus had found a fantastic home. I looked up at Mr Bellerby, who was now clutching the lamb.

"Oh yes. He's definitely settled in all reet!" He beamed. "He'll be rounding up sheep in no time. He's lovely and, of course, he's my new best friend."

A Christmas Delivery

Christmas Eve was always a great time at the
practice. Half the vets worked over Christmas
and the other half over New Year, but by
Christmas Eve, routine work was postponed
until January, so the feeling of "emergencies
only" was always quite exciting.

As afternoon surgery came to an end, I was still waiting for a phone call from the laboratory with some important results for a case I'd been treating. I really needed them before everything closed for the holiday period. Eventually, the phone rang and Sylvia, the receptionist, answered.

"Julian," she called, "I've got Rudolf on the phone. Can he have a word with you?"

Rudolf was the scientist who worked at the laboratory, calling with the lab results. A lady waiting with her dog in reception overheard part of the conversation and she let out a jolly chuckle. Of course, she didn't know that Rudolf was the name of the laboratory vet and, in festive spirits, put two and two together to make five.

"Oh, my goodness!" she exclaimed. "You'd better get going! We don't want Rudolf to be poorly on Christmas Eve. I expect he's got a problem with his nose? I hope you manage to get him fixed!"

"We'll do our best," I said with a smile. "Goodnight and Happy Christmas!"

As the last client of the afternoon headed off, I pushed the on-call bleeper into my pocket, whistled to Emmy and together we headed home, ready for whatever the next few days might bring.

When the call came, it was urgent and caught me off guard. I was fast asleep. I peered at the illuminated numbers on the clock beside my bed – it was exactly two o'clock in the morning.

Calving problems. Older cow. Visit please, Greenfield Farm – my pager told me everything I needed to know. I'd been to Greenfield Farm almost every day over the previous few weeks, as their heifers and cows had been struggling to give birth by themselves. Heifers are young cows who are giving birth to their first calves, which is usually difficult for first-time mums. Older cows who have calved before tended to have fewer issues, so I knew there must be a serious problem. A combination of some very rich and nutritious hay and the recent cold weather had caused the cattle to fill their hungry bellies with extra food. It was the best way to keep warm, but it had also made their unborn calves grow much bigger than usual and almost every one needed veterinary assistance to be born.

So, on this night before Christmas, while Santa was busily delivering presents, a vet in snowy North Yorkshire would be delivering something quite different. I hoped the outcome would put just as big a smile on the farmer's face as Santa would upon the faces of children all over the world.

I crept downstairs, past Emmy, who was enjoying a nice cosy sleep in her basket under the Christmas tree. I smiled to myself as the baubles twinkled in the moonlight. Emmy lifted her head at the sound of my approach.

"You stay here, Em," I whispered as I pulled on my wellies and thick coat.

She lowered her head obligingly and closed her eyes. How I wished I could go back to bed too! The calving was sure to be a challenge, especially in the small hours of Christmas Day, but the journey to get there would be just as hard. Winter had a stiff hold on Yorkshire this year. Fields, hedges and roads had been iced over ever since my fateful visit to Hagg Farm, where I'd skidded on the ice and crashed my car into the hedge.

The wild tops of the nearby hills are often white during winter, but snowdrifts are seldom seen on the sheltered low ground of the valley bottoms. This winter, though, was particularly harsh and iron-hard frozen land had been white for over a month. Although it was freezing, and exposed ears and fingers quickly ached with the cold, everyone working outside had become accustomed to the polar conditions. Farmers and vets carried on as best they could in the difficult winter months.

The gritting lorries hadn't reached the road to Greenfield Farm, so it was covered in compressed snow, with a treacherous icy surface. I'd learnt that it was only safe to travel on lanes like this at very low speeds and that you should never to make sudden changes of direction. In the crisp darkness, it was slow progress.

When I eventually arrived, I inched cautiously across the frosted farmyard, parking as close as I could to the cowshed. The farmers, John and his wife, Joan, were waiting for me. They must have seen my headlights in the distance as I approached. They were wrapped up in layers of coats and jumpers, with scarves and hats bundled over the top, so that I barely recognized them.

The wind swirled from time to time,

spinning snow into spirals. It was a beautiful but bitter night. With a couple of cows quietly peering over the gate to see what was going on, the scene was almost straight out of a nativity play. There were even wooden hay mangers, though admittedly without a baby inside.

"Happy Christmas," I said as I got out of the car.

"Merry Christmas," said John and Joan in unison. They didn't sound very merry though. "It's another tough one, I'm afraid," added John.

"Ho ho ho!" I chuckled. "I'm here to deliver a special present – a calf!" Neither of them laughed. They didn't even smile. They just shuffled off into the fold yard.

"She's in 'ere," explained Joan, completely ignoring my attempted joke. She showed me into the cowshed, where about twenty huge cows huddled together in the far corner. Snow lay in the front part of the shed, blown in through gaps near the door and between the wooden slats.

I shivered at the thought of taking off my shirt, which is my usual habit when I calve a cow. It might seem a peculiar thing to do, but it allows me to use my whole arm, without a rolled-up sleeve getting in the way, and it saves a shirt from being ruined.

The cows were silent tonight. Some were curled up asleep, dotted around on the straw in places away from the snow. Others quietly chewed their cud, with their mouths moving from side to side in a rhythmic fashion. Steam was rising from each one with every breath. It was a peaceful sight and I paused for a moment to take it in.

Farmyards have a special smell of their own. Like the sweet and fruity pear-drop scent of silage – grass that's been preserved to use as cattle feed during the cold winter months. It's a unique smell, and one to which I have become very accustomed. It was quite different from the typical Christmassy smells of pine needles and cinnamon, but to me, it was just as lovely and I breathed it in deeply, readying myself for the task at hand.

"That's her. Over there. In the corner,"
John said plainly, pointing to the expectant
cow. "We call her Buttercup." She was
standing alone – something cows like to
do when they are preparing to give birth.
Buttercup's tail pointed straight out behind
her and two large feet protruded from
underneath the pointed tail.

They belonged to the unborn calf, which, judging from the size of the feet, would be another whopper.

"How long's she been on for, John?" I asked. This was an important question. If Buttercup was very early on in the process of giving birth, it could be that she just needed more time. But if the mother had been struggling for a while, she might need a little more help. I could tell from the two feet I could see that the calf was facing the right way round. What I couldn't tell was if there was a head lined up nicely behind them.

"Since midnight," John confirmed. "I checked them, and she was just thinking about it, so I decided to give her a couple of hours. I hoped she'd have done it herself. She's a good cow and she's had plenty of calves before. But it's gonna be a big 'un, I think, so I wanted you to come and help her."

There was already a bucket of warm water ready for me, with steam pluming from the surface. Everything was ready.

"Will she stand?" I asked. "Or should we get a halter on her?"

"I think she'll stand," said Joan. "She's a quiet cow, but we'll walk her behind that gate to keep her still."

Despite her imminent problems, Buttercup obligingly wandered to her place behind the gate, which John pulled round to keep her still. I couldn't put it off any longer. I took a deep breath, then peeled off the layers of warm clothes on my upper body. I added some gel to my hand then inserted my arm as far as my elbow, until I could reach up and around the wedged calf.

Its feet and knuckle joints were worryingly large, but thankfully not crossed over. The discovery of crossed feet at this point is a sure sign that the calf will be too big to fit through and signals the need to operate to get the calf out safely. This was encouraging news and I felt further inside.

The head was there too, but tilted to one side as if the calf were cocking its head, like Emmy would do when I spoke to her. Emmy's little face briefly flashed in my mind. I was looking forward to bringing the calf safely into the world, then heading home for Christmas breakfast with Emmy.

I worked my hand behind the calf's head and down the neck towards its body, trying to decide whether there would be enough space. The calf was very large, but I judged that there would just about be room – if only I could straighten the calf!

"The head's twisted, John. I'll need to straighten it up, but if I can, I reckon it will come," I said optimistically.

John nodded with approval. "Whatever you think. You're the boss. I can help give a pull if you need."

I had already poured some antiseptic into the bucket of steaming water, along with my calving ropes and sticks. Calving sticks are short pieces of wood that you can use as a handle when pulling on the rope. It's no good pulling hard on the ropes by themselves, because they dig painfully into your hands and are often too slippery to hold on to properly, so it's important to have calving sticks to hand.

I was some way from needing the sticks or John's help just yet though, because the next job was to straighten out the calf's head. First, I attached a rope to each foot, above the carpus (the equivalent of our wrist) and gave a firm and steady pull, to make sure the legs were fully extended.

Next, I inserted both my hands and grasped the calf's head near its ears. I tried to twist it gently, as it needed to be upright. Buttercup, who had been behaving impeccably so far, let out a low moaning noise, obviously feeling that things were starting to move.

Soon, after some steady manipulations, the calf's head was almost up to where I needed it, but then Buttercup started to push. Unfortunately, this had the opposite effect to what I'd hoped, forcing the head back to its original position. I tried again, but the same thing happened, and this time she let out an even louder moo!

"Easy, girl," I said, standing away from the cow. I gave her a reassuring pat on her flank. "It's not going to be easy, I'm afraid. I'll need a head rope," I explained as I turned back to John and Joan.

Attaching a head rope is quite difficult. Working with my fingertips, I loop the rope over the calf's ears and into its mouth, a bit like a bridle for a horse. It's no good just looping it around the neck, because this can choke the poor calf. Using a head rope doesn't hurt the calf at all, but it needs to be precise and is often fiddly, which is made more challenging if the patient fidgets.

All this in a dark barn on a freezing night. But I had no option. It had to be done…

Joan edged towards Buttercup and whispered soothingly to her as I got to work again. After a long struggle, with beads of sweat forming on my forehead even in sub-zero temperatures, I finally managed to secure the rope around the calf's head.

"Got it!" I exclaimed with renewed hope. "John, can you apply some steady pressure to this rope while I get the head into position?"

With John's help, the calf's head was straightening up nicely, but we weren't out of the woods yet. Now I had to think about getting the calf out safely.

It was often a delicate balance of technique, strength and judgement. Could I get it out? I really hoped so. If I failed, Christmas might be ruined for John and his wife. And as well as the mother, I had a cow byre full of animal onlookers also as expectant as Mum. More than ever, the pressure was on!

Finally, our combined efforts appeared to have succeeded and everything was in position. Now we needed to loop a rope around each of the calf's legs. With this and the one on its head, we just had to hope Mum had sufficient strength to push while we pulled. She was an experienced cow and I was hopeful she'd know what to do.

I reached for the calving sticks and slipped a rope onto each leg.

"Here you go, John," I said, passing him one of the sticks. "Let's take it steady and see what happens."

This was the moment of truth. We dug our heels into the straw to get a good grip and leant backwards, away from the cow. We made steady progress, with Joan offering some words of encouragement to Buttercup and to us.

"Cush, cush, old girl. You're doing well," she said, patting her flank. John and I were huffing and puffing behind. We were doing well, too, I thought. The calf's nose had appeared into the frosty world.

"Hold it there, John. I need to feel round the back of the calf's head now."

I let go of my rope and stick, and had another feel beyond the calf's head.

It was crucial to work out if there was enough space for the calf's body to follow the head and front legs. It would be a disaster if the head emerged, but the rest of the body couldn't fit. It was time for another big decision.

"I think this'll come, John," I declared with confidence. "Let's get back to the ropes. If we can just get the head out, I'm pretty sure the rest will follow."

We pulled again. Buttercup pushed again. There was more noise from all three of us, and I glanced across the cowshed. Quite a few of the cows were awake now and seemed to be watching what was going on, although the sleeping ones were still curled up and oblivious to the whole situation.

Joan continued her soothing words and then, with a huge moo from Mum, the calf's head emerged, closely followed by two slippery ears. The newborn opened its eyes, blinked and looked around. Then, with one last pull and push, the huge calf landed safely on the soft straw.

John and I fell backwards, almost on top of each other! We both laughed as we landed in the straw.

"Happy Christmas!" I said for the second time that morning, this time from my comfy straw bed.

"By Jove! That's a cracking Christmas present if ever I saw one!" John laughed.

He was right. It had been a good night's work and we had succeeded, despite the cold. Joan quickly rushed off and returned with a fresh bucket of water and I was thankful for its warmth. As I washed my arms and upper body, I looked over at Buttercup and her new calf, watching the mother lovingly lick her calf all over – the start of a maternal bond that would last a lifetime. It was a happy scene and again I thought about the nativity.

"All we need now is Three Wise Men!" I joked. This time, everybody laughed.

Smartie on the Moor

It was a wintry afternoon, with darkness
approaching. As the wind picked up,
bringing with it the threat of snow, it seemed
absurd to be out on the moors. But I had
received an emergency call. Mr Barnby's
pony was stuck in a ditch on the moorland.
I had no choice but to head out into the dark
to help with a rescue attempt.

I felt like a medieval knight embarking on a dangerous quest as I drove slowly towards the moors with Emmy and Mr Barnby as passengers. We trundled slowly up a track until it ran out beside a tumbledown drystone wall. The wall marked the upper edge of the low pastures, with an expanse of rough moorland above. But it had seen better days and clearly didn't offer a secure boundary for any sort of livestock – and certainly not Fell ponies, who roamed the high moorlands known as fells.

"That's as far as we can get on wheels. We'll 'ave to walk the rest of the way," said Mr Barnby in a matter-of-fact way, pointing into the far distance.

"OK. Is it a long way?" I asked cautiously. I'd been to his farm on a number of occasions, but always to treat cows in one of the stone buildings that surrounded the farmhouse, next to the milking parlour. I'd never had cause to venture onto the moors, their edge marked by sharp, vertical gritstone rock faces that cast dark shadows over the pastures below.

Even on a pleasant summer's day, the moors looked menacing and bleak, but at the same time they were beautiful. I loved their rugged solitude. On a sunny day, my eyes were always drawn up towards them, and on a rare day off I would often head out to explore them on my bike or on foot with Emmy, my ever-enthusiastic companion.

"Oh, it's not far," Mr Barnby reassured me, although I wasn't completely convinced his idea of "not far" would be the same as mine. "Smartie's just up there, round that corner. It's not such a long distance away." He paused for a moment, before adding, "Problem is, the ground gets awful rough up there. T'old girl's at the bottom of a bank and it's reet steep."

Any hope I had of this call being a simple job immediately evaporated. Before we left the shelter of the yard, I considered all the equipment I might need to examine and treat the poor pony, running through all the possibilities in my head. The last thing I wanted was to have to retrace my steps across the edge of a wild moorland on a winter night, if I'd forgotten to bring anything. At this rate, any steps I made would soon be covered in snow, so there was no guarantee that I'd even be able to find my way back.

As I double-checked I had everything I needed, I looked up to the sky, where the clouds were gathering overhead. To the west, the last of the sun was slipping rapidly towards the horizon. We didn't have long before night fell. I reckoned no more than an hour.

I refocused on packing my equipment into a large bucket – syringes, needles and bottles of medicine to cover most possible outcomes. I added a small bottle of liquid paraffin and some Epsom salts, just in case the pony was suffering from stomach pains known as colic. As an afterthought, I picked up a hoof knife and pushed it into my pocket. The curved knife, with its sculpted wooden handle, had been passed down to me from an experienced farrier – someone who makes and fits horse shoes – as a thank you for helping him out in the past. I liked the feel of it in my hand and the blade was very sharp. It would help me explore the pony's foot if necessary.

"Smartie's an old girl, but she's a tough 'un," explained Mr Barnby as we abandoned the car and clambered through a gap in the stone wall. "She never wants to come inside to the warm. Not even in bad weather like this.

I call her in and give her hay, which she loves,
mind you, but she bangs on the stable door to
be out, even in winter. I let her 'ave her way
during the day, but I make sure she comes in
overnight. That's when I realized there was
a problem. I called her, but she didn't come,
you see, so I went looking on the moors."

As the farmer marched ahead resolutely,
I struggled to keep up, let alone continue a
conversation. Emmy was happily keeping
pace with Mr Barnby, but I was carrying a

heavy bucket of equipment and wearing my
usual cumbersome wellies and waterproof
trousers, so it was hard going. We were
crossing the shoulder of a steep hill.
The terrain underfoot was rough, uneven
and semi-frozen. As we continued on,
I couldn't help but feel out of breath. I was
pretty fit and quite accustomed to hard effort,
but the farmer did this route every day, so he
was very used to the pathless ground, even in
the difficult conditions.

"How long do you think she's been there for?" I puffed.

"She could have been there most of the day," came the anxious reply. "I opened her stable door after I'd finished milking the cows at first light. I 'aven't seen her since then. The worst bit is, she's really Emily's pony – that's my daughter. She learnt to ride on her. She's not back from school yet and she doesn't know there's a problem. I hope you can get her fixed, 'cos she'll be devastated if you can't get her right."

Treating a pony stuck in a ditch on the steep side of a wild and increasingly dark moor was going to be hard enough. But that she was the beloved companion of a young girl raised the stakes still more. And we hadn't even found her yet.

"I'll do my best, Mr Barnby," I said, between gasps for breath.

Underfoot, the sheep-grazed grass had given way to rough tussock grass with boggy, semi-frozen patches, occasional clumps of heather and brown bracken made crispy by frosts. It was at times like these that I wondered why I'd decided to become a vet. There were many easier jobs, with predictable hours and simpler tasks. Luckily, I didn't have much longer to ponder this thought, as the black-and-white form of a stocky pony came into view. Smartie was motionless and lying in an unusual place further down by a small stream. I could immediately tell that the situation was serious.

"There she is. It doesn't look good, does it?" Mr Barnby said.

"Well, let me get a closer look," I replied. "There's a lot that could be going on."

I surveyed the scene. Smartie was

apparently unable to move. She must have been there for a while, because the boggy ground underneath her had turned from grass to mud, and the bracken had been completely flattened in a rough circle under her weight. Scrapings in the ground showed that she'd been struggling to get up, and the bruised skin under her chin and along her jawline told a similar story.

She was a few metres away from the shallow stream, with small rowan trees along its bank. Higher up, the stream trickled more quickly through a steep rocky gully from the moors above. Could she have fallen down there? *Maybe she's broken her leg?* I wondered. I'd seen this sort of accident before, with ungainly young thoroughbreds slipping on close-cropped wet grass. But Smartie was a tough Fell pony. Surely she was more sure-footed than that?

I crouched by her and patted her on the
neck as Mr Barnby knelt down to cradle
her sore head on his lap. Even Emmy stood
near Smartie, as if she were protecting her.
Smartie let out a soft whinny in appreciation.

Stage one of our challenge was complete
– we'd found the patient. Next, I had to
find out what was the matter. I set about my
examination, starting by feeling the lower
part of Smartie's limbs. Each one was firm

and intact, so I was confident there were no serious fractures. I breathed a sigh.

"I can't feel anything broken," I reported. "I was worried she might have a break, especially when you look up there, at that steep cliff."

Next, I plugged my stethoscope into my ears so that I could listen to Smartie's heartbeat and breathing.

Her heart rate was high, which meant that she might be in pain. Poor Smartie! Her lungs sounded clear, though her breathing was shallow and rapid. I moved my stethoscope further down her body, which was sweating despite the chill of the early evening air. Now I listened hard to the noises in her stomach. Too much gurgling, or worse, no gurgling at all, might indicate a blockage or twisting in her intestines – a sure sign of colic.

I moved the stethoscope to different

points on her upper side – everything was normal. Intermittent gurgling, every twenty or thirty seconds. With difficulty, I pushed the end of the stethoscope under her to the other side, squashed between her skin and the fell-side underneath.

"Everything sounds pretty normal, Mr Barnby," I reported again. "That's good news, but I'm a bit perplexed. I felt sure there would be some form of colic. It's the most likely thing to make a horse suddenly go down. And her heart rate is very high, so it's obvious something is bothering her. I just can't find the cause."

Emmy tilted her head inquisitively. I wondered if she was puzzled too.

I checked Smartie's temperature, which again was normal, and scratched my head. "I'm sure it's the pain that's stopping her from getting up, so I'll give her a dose of painkiller.

It'll work quickly and that will help. But I still really need to find out the cause."

Mr Barnby nodded as I found a syringe and needle and prepared the medication. I gently searched for Smartie's jugular vein, which was easy to find, flowing like a drainpipe along the underside of her neck. As I injected the full syringe, Smartie made a small neighing noise, which made her nostrils flare. Her breath was warm and the cloud of vapour it formed in the cold air made her look like a tired dragon.

After a few minutes, all of a sudden and without warning, Smartie started to move. She lifted her head and looked around, as if to work out where she was. With encouragement from the farmer and me, she hobbled to her feet, wobbling all the time but concentrating hard on staying upright.

"Well, look at that!" Mr Barnby exclaimed,

clapping his gloved hands together. "It's like a miracle!"

It was certainly encouraging, but there was better news for me. Now Smartie was on her feet, the source of her pain became obvious. Her front left foot hung limp, hardly touching the ground. It must have been very sore. I bent over, feeling the hoof with my muddy hands. The hoof wall was warm – something I hadn't noticed before – and there was a throbbing pulse on the lower part of the leg, above the foot. This was a sure sign of a condition where fluid builds under the leathery sole of the foot – a condition known as "pus in the foot". No wonder Smartie couldn't get up!

There was only one thing I could do to really help her. I needed to release the trapped fluid so that she could put weight on her foot again. I found the hoof knife in my pocket and lifted Smartie's sore foot, securing it between my knees. I always found this tricky to do on the flat floor of a stable, but on the sloping, snow-covered hillside, it felt even more precarious.

I prodded the sole, searching for the painful area, and quickly found a soft, discoloured part of the hoof. Smartie jerked her head, confirming, I thought, that this was the spot. Very carefully, I began to slice thin slivers of sole away. Amazingly, horses don't feel this at all – it's like trimming a human's toenails! The hoof knife had a curved end, allowing precise carving. With each slice, Smartie lifted her head, and I knew I was getting closer to the painful trapped fluid.

"Steady, Smartie. I'm nearly there," I said encouragingly. Smartie was starting to react against me holding her foot – her increasing discomfort suggested I was almost at the source of the pain. "Just a couple more, I think, Mr Barnby," I added, encouraging the farmer too. He was holding Smartie's head collar and couldn't see my progress.

Just two more gentle slices and suddenly a jet of dark grey liquid shot out of Smartie's foot! She shuddered in a mixture of pain and relief, suddenly feeling comfortable. But she'd had enough of my poking about. She shook her mane disapprovingly and stamped her foot down.

"That's better – look!" Mr Barnby exclaimed. "She's standing on it already."

The combination of the painkillers and the release of the pressure in Smartie's foot quickly returned the tough pony to her old self. Or, at least, very nearly. She looked around in the deepening gloom – the winter sun had almost gone now – and snorted a few times as if to say, "That feels much better!

How did I get here in the first place? I think it's time to go back home now."

Emmy agreed and started to trot back down the uneven slope.

"Shall we head back then?" I asked.

Mr Barnby nodded. He held Smartie's head collar and steered her across the rough moor and onto the narrow track as we retraced our steps. At the top of the pasture, I clambered into my car and turned on the headlights. I was swiftly followed by Emmy, and slowly crawled along with the window down, chatting to Mr Barnby, who led the pony steadily back towards the farm.

By now the sky was dark, but the lights were on in the farm buildings below. They looked warm and inviting, even for a pony accustomed to windswept fells. Suddenly, a little girl came into view, running from the farmhouse.

"Look, it's Emily. She'll have just got home from school," the farmer said.

Emily rushed across the yard and flung her arms around Smartie's neck.

"Is she all right?" she asked me, her face buried deeply in the pony's shaggy mane.

"Yes, she'll be fine, I'm sure," I reassured the worried little girl. "Although Smartie was in quite a pickle. She was very lucky that your dad found her, especially on such a cold night."

"Thank you," she said and hugged her father tightly.

"She'll need some more treatment," I said. "Something you can help with, I think. Now, could I have a bucket of very warm water, please?"

Emily nodded and ran off to fetch the water. Smartie would need regular bandages on her foot, with special dressings underneath to clean, protect and encourage the infection to drain from the depths of her foot. I would need to show Emily what was needed.

"Here you go," she said as she put the bucket down next to Smartie.

"Thank you. OK, you'll need to do this twice a day, and you'll need Dad to help you lift Smartie's foot" I explained. "Cut this bandage into a square about the size of her foot, then soak it in hot water. Next, place it with the smooth side against the sole, then wrap it up and bandage it in place with this stretchy tape."

Emily watched intently and nodded. Smartie stood still and didn't object. She was reassured that Emily was around and I think the pony knew we were helping her.

"I'll do it like you say, if it will make Smartie feel better."

"It will. Just remember, do it twice a day, and I'll come back at the weekend and have another look to see how she's doing."

It was completely dark by the time I said goodbye to Smartie, Mr Barnby and Emily. As I drove down the farm track, I could just see them in my rear mirror, lit up by the orange glowing lights from within the old stone stable. Mr Barnby was still waving when I reached the road. And Emily was clinging to her pony, standing on tiptoes with her arms wrapped around Smartie's strong neck. Smartie had a mouthful of hay and looked happy to be back home and safe, pleased for once to be in a secure stable.

It had been a challenging afternoon – even poor Emmy was pleased to be safely back off the dark moor. She curled up contentedly on the passenger seat. But it had also been a successful and fortunate day. I felt sure Smartie was over the worst of her problems and in good hands. I couldn't wait to come back and see her at the weekend, in a warm, well-lit stable, and hopefully feeling a lot, lot better.

Yes, sometimes it was tough being a vet, clambering onto a wild moor under a menacing sky, and there were definitely easier ways to earn a living. But, for me on this evening, being a vet was all I wanted to be doing – my dream job.

The Lost Parakeet

It was a grey day in February when a mysterious shoebox arrived with a brightly coloured parakeet inside. He'd been found in a school playground and the person who had rescued him had done well to capture the little bird and transfer him into the box. Everyone knows that a school playground in Yorkshire is not the usual habitat for a colourful parakeet.

"The name's James," I'm sure the bird muttered as he sat on my shoulder in the isolation ward of the practice. The words were not very clear, and I had to strain my ears to make them out. Was that really what he was saying? It was hard to be certain. The colourful parakeet was as talkative as he had been lucky, although I was beginning to realize that he was also very mischievous. Right now, this was the only information we had about the parakeet, who (I was fairly certain) had introduced himself as James.

After checking him over in case he was injured, my plan was to secure him safely in a kennel. If he had escaped already, there was a good chance he would try and do the same again. Already he'd forced his way out of a small gap in the shoebox in which he had arrived and made himself comfortable, on my shoulder, like a pirate's tiny parrot.

This sort of thing doesn't happen very often, so I made the most of the opportunity, saying pirate expressions like "shiver me timbers" to the nurses who walked past. Surprisingly, they didn't seem to find it as amusing as I did. I rounded it all off with one of my favourite jokes: "James, do you know why pirates are called pirates?"

The little bird cocked his head to one side, looked quizzical and said, "Helloooo," but nothing else. Either he couldn't understand me, or he'd heard the joke so many times he couldn't be bothered to reply.

"Because they argh," I said, laughing to myself.

Not one of my colleagues thought this joke was funny and neither did James. He immediately took flight, flapping around the prep room in circles close to the ceiling. Nurses and other vets ducked

and swerved to avoid the swooping bird.
He seemed to be enjoying his adventure,
apparently searching for a window or door
to fly through. I guessed he hadn't been
to a veterinary surgery before. He seemed
excited to be able to view it from all angles.
Maybe he was looking for other animals who
he might be able to befriend and talk to?

"Argh!" came a shriek. It wasn't anyone
pretending to be a pirate. It came from Tracy,
the practice manager, who had come down
from the office to investigate the source of
all the commotion. Tracy loves dogs, their
owners and spreadsheets (in that order), but
not birds. Especially not birds on the loose.

James swooped past, startling Tracy and emitting a jet of poo that narrowly missed the clipboard she was carrying!

"That's not very nice, James!" I shouted. "Come back here!"

I rushed to the rescue, reaching out with both hands, quickly but carefully. But James was much too fast. I floundered and missed. I sought assistance from Lucy the nurse. With twice as much human power, we waved our arms and made noises, and eventually managed to waft him into the safety of the isolation ward. This was a much smaller space, where we stood a better chance of cornering this escape artist with wings.

There were two kennels in the small room, one above the other. Usually, anxious or infectious patients were placed there away from other animals, so they were not too frightened or wouldn't risk passing on infection. Today, though, it was my own dog, Emmy, who was waiting in the lower kennel, having found her way in here away from all the chaos. She was confused by the arrival of a colourful bird and cocked her ears, watching it intently. She was used to seeing pigeons in the garden at home, squirrels and other creatures when on walks in the woods, but I'm sure she'd never seen a green, red and yellow bird who could talk.

I pondered how best to get James back into his box.

Luckily, he came to me, perching himself on my shoulder again, which seemed to be his favourite place. Both the parakeet and I were really quite enjoying all this, but Emmy wasn't. She looked distinctly indignant that the little bird was competing for my attention and affection as he chattered away in my ear. I couldn't understand anything he was saying, but he carried on anyway.

From his perch on my shoulder, it was a fairly simple task to pop James into the kennel, where he could be safely secured. While I really wanted to continue our new friendship, it was clear I wouldn't get much work done with a small parrot on my shoulder. Especially one that kept flying off and frightening the staff. I also thought that James must have an actual owner – he was very accustomed to human company. I imagined that someone, somewhere, must be very worried.

The first step towards reuniting James with his owner involved a post on social media, which included a photo.

Lost parakeet. Very colourful. Handed into the vet's this morning. Possibly called James.

Tracy pressed "send" and we all crossed our fingers. Then I turned to the parakeet. "James," I said, "I'm going to have to go now because I've got a busy day. First on my list is a Border collie with a lump to be removed from his leg."

James tilted his head to one side. I waited for a reply, expecting something along the lines of "What's a Border collie?" Or "What's a lump?" Or even "What's a leg?" That sounded like the sort of question an inquisitive parakeet might ask.

"Hello! The name's James," he seemed to say again, nodding his head. I wasn't entirely sure he understood anything about Border collies or lumps. Or legs, for that matter.

"OK, James. I'll be back soon. In the meantime, you have some apple pieces and some raisins to eat. I hope you like them."

The lump on the collie proved easy to remove and the patient was soon back in his own kennel with a few stitches in his front leg under a huge red bandage, brighter than James himself.

As soon as the dog was fully awake, I returned to check on the bird. He was a confident little chap, but watching him sitting alone in his cage, I felt sorry for him. James was busy eating his snacks, but quickly stopped what he was doing when I opened the cage door. James opened his beak and a raisin fell out. I hoped for another conversation, but James wasn't in the mood for talking this time and picked up a juicy piece of apple instead.

"How are you doing, James?" I asked, half expecting an answer. "I'm just off to see a sheep, then I have some other birds to see, would you believe? Some peacocks and peahens with sore eyes! I'd love to take you with me to see them, but it's probably better that you stay here. It'll be safer, I think."

Again, the little bird dropped his food, tilted his head to one side and replied, "Hello! The name's James."

"Bye, James. I'll be back soon. Hopefully you might have remembered some new words by then! Try not to frighten Tracy. And DO NOT escape!"

I closed the cage, then whistled to Emmy.

"Come on, Em, you can come with me. I've got some calls to do." As fast as an escaping parrot, Emmy rushed out. She loved coming with me on my calls and she scuttled along at high speed and leapt into the car.

On the way to Greenfield Farm, I told her all about the mini parrot, what he'd been saying and how he'd arrived at the practice. Emmy looked at me inquisitively, before turning her attention to the view out of the window as we approached the farm.

It had been a long winter for the farmers. The lambing had been tricky and the cows had all had very big calves. But now, the calves were all strong and healthy and it was the turn of the sheep to take centre stage.

Most sheep have their lambs in February and March, with just some breeds – like those at Hagg Farm and Mr Bellerby's – having them earlier in the winter. At this time of the year, it is much more usual for a vet to be lambing a sheep than talking to a parakeet! Sore and chapped hands and increasing levels of exhaustion are the norm, but it's a season that we all love.

Working with sheep is great, and delivering the lamb at Greenfield Farm was as rewarding as always.

"By Jove! That was a tight one, Julian," John the farmer said when I'd finally manoeuvred the lamb out into the world. "That's a very lucky lamb."

It was a lucky lamb and I felt the usual sense of satisfaction as we watched the lamb totter to its feet, looking for Mum's milk. The miracle of life amazed me, yet again.

Before I knew it, I was back in the car with Emmy on our way to visit some poorly peacocks and peahens. The birds had gluey, swollen eyes and their temperatures were high. I knew their recovery would be slow. I made sure I wore protective gloves as I examined each one and administered drops to the painful eyes. I didn't want to risk passing the eye infection on to James.

Peacock diseases, I felt sure, could easily spread to parakeets.

By the time I arrived back at the surgery, Tracy had some good news.

"We've found the owners!" she exclaimed joyfully as I came through the back door. "They're coming to collect him later this afternoon, so he'll be with us for a bit longer. Maybe you can encourage James to say something other than 'Hello'!"

"That's a relief, I bet they were worried," I replied. "And maybe I can teach James how to say goodbye!"

It turned out that James belonged to a little boy called Archie. It was Archie's mum who had seen our message and called straight away. She was delighted that James had been found. Archie was still at school, so a plan had been made to collect the escapee on their way home. Until then, we had a lively, colourful and mischievous parakeet for company. Happy in the knowledge that he'd be safely back home soon, I wasted no time in telling him the news and all about the unfortunate peacocks and peahens and the lucky lamb.

"James, we've found your owner," I said triumphantly. But James seemed oblivious to the good news and hopped up onto the upturned shoebox we had put in his kennel as a perch. Was James too busy enjoying his apple pieces and raisins? There is a well-known phrase about communicating with animals:

"If only they could talk…" But in James's case, I knew he could talk. Maybe he just couldn't understand?

Later that day, after school had finished, a relieved mother and her excited son, Archie, arrived in the waiting room. I called them into my consulting room to hear the story of how the little parrot had got lost. I also found that he wasn't called James at all. His name was Seb.

"I'm so glad you've found him!" said Archie's mum with tears of relief. "He escaped from the kitchen this morning while I was taking in the shopping from the car. The door was open and I hadn't realized Seb was out of his birdcage. He's such a friendly little bird and he always likes to sit on a shoulder when I'm doing jobs around the house. All day I've been worried about what I'd say when Archie came home from school. I have been hoping against hope that Seb would come back."

I explained that someone had managed to catch him and put him in a box to bring him into us, as people often do with lost and found animals. It was at this point that Tracy appeared.

"Someone from the school down the road at Three Lane Ends found him," she explained. "He was flying around the playground, then landed on the gate. I think it was the headmaster who brought him in, because he was very smartly dressed."

"That's my school!" Archie exclaimed with excitement and a large grin on his face. "Seb must have flown out of the kitchen and followed me to school!"

"Well, he's certainly an adventurous chap," I said, but now it was time to reunite Archie and Seb. "I'll go and get him then."

I went off to the isolation ward that had been the parakeet's home for the day. Emmy woke up from her sleep in a comfy bed in the kennel below and looked at me expectantly.

"It's Seb I need, Em. Sorry. You need to wait here a bit longer before home time," I told her, before turning to the parakeet. "Time for you to go home, Seb!"

I hoped he might burst into conversation now that I'd finally got his name right, but he just cocked his head again and said, "Hello!" I was about to open the kennel door and carefully put the little bird back into the shoebox, but then I had an idea.

"Lucy, are all the doors and windows closed?" I called.

"Yes, thankfully," the nurse replied from the prep room, "Why? What's your plan?"

I opened the kennel and Seb hopped out, flew around the little room twice and then landed on my shoulder. I walked slowly and cautiously towards the consulting room, where Archie and his mum were waiting. This was unusual, because most patients come and go in a basket (if they're a cat or rabbit), on a lead (if they're a dog or a small pig) or in a box (if they're a tortoise or hedgehog). It's safer that way.

This afternoon, though, I knew it would be pretty safe to let the bird out. Seb had flown from his home all the way to Archie's school to find him. I was pretty certain – so long as the doors and windows were closed – that the plucky little bird would fly straight from my shoulder to be reunited with his best friend.

"Look who's here, Seb," I said as we approached the half-open door.

As soon as Seb spotted Archie, he took off and made a beeline directly to the shoulder of the little boy.

"Hello! The name's James," Seb said, his head bobbing up and down with excitement.

"Archie, what is he saying?" I asked. "He obviously isn't called James. I've been listening to him chatting all day. I've tried to understand him, but I'm confused."

"Well, I'm confused too!" Archie laughed. "Sometimes I think he knows exactly what he's saying. Other times he doesn't have a clue. Last week I'm sure he said, 'I like lasagne.' But he's never even tasted lasagne, so it can't have been that!"

"Hang on," I said to Archie. "What's the name of your headmaster?"

"It's Mr James." Archie smiled. "That must be it! Mr James must have said hello to Archie when he rescued him."

We quickly agreed that Seb had been trying to let us know about Mr James all along. What a clever little bird he was after all!

Seb also knew where he wanted to be, and that was with his beloved owner, Archie. That was all that really mattered.

Seb started chatting excitedly to Archie, still mostly about lasagne and Mr James. The parakeet was clearly delighted to be reunited with his owner. But Archie turned to me to continue some human conversation.

"Thank you for looking after him," he said politely. "I have a feeling this won't be the last time you see him at your surgery!"

"You're very welcome," I said. "Let's hope he doesn't make another escape. Although I have to say, we've all enjoyed his visit today."

Everyone at the practice (well, maybe everyone except Tracy) was very much looking forward to Seb and Archie's next visit, but we hoped it would be under less worrying circumstances – maybe for a nail or beak trim.

The afternoon was drawing to an end as we all lined up to wave goodbye to Seb, Archie and his mum. It had been another busy day, but Seb had brightened it with his energy, escape antics and lovely colourful feathers. They certainly more than made up for his terrible conversation!

The Orphan Alpaca

There was another emergency at Jackie's farm. But it was very different from my last visit because today, despite the drama that surely lay ahead, I felt energized by the possibility that winter might finally be behind me.

The sun was bright, and the air was clean and fresh. Shoots of grass glowing with new life had grown up through the sticky mud in fields and on farm tracks. The sun's rays had enough power that, so long as I stayed still for long enough, there was a hint of warmth on my skin. I rolled up my sleeves. The darkest and coldest days were over, and surely spring was on its way.

If I knew how to whistle properly, I would have been making a cheerful tune as I drove around the familiar lanes with Emmy sitting beside me. The arrival of spring brought an uplifting feeling for everyone. But for those of us who spent much of the time working outside, warmer, drier weather with longer and brighter days was especially welcome. It was a time of optimism and happiness.

But any ideas of relaxing in the sun would have to wait. I had another challenge ahead and I needed to hurry. There was a big problem with a little alpaca.

"Cinderella is trying to give birth," Jackie had said over the phone. "But there's something seriously wrong with her."

This brought back memories of the first time I'd met Cinderella. That too was a birth-related problem. The cria (a baby alpaca) was positioned the wrong way round. I'd had a tough time unfolding its back legs, which were tangled like a well-used ball of wool. Jackie suspected a similar problem today, but surely the same thing couldn't happen again? I hoped not.

When I arrived at the farm, the herd was grazing quietly, enjoying the sun and new grass. Jackie's fields sloped gently towards the valley below, and I took in the perfect view of the alpacas on one side and the beauty of Yorkshire on the other as I made my way along the farm track. It was particularly pleasant today, with green fields, blue sky and bright white clouds.

The herd was peacefully unaware that one of their friends was inside the barn, pacing around uncomfortably. Alpacas are sociable and curious creatures, and often gather around to examine anything unusual. But today, it looked as though they were preoccupied with the warmer weather, lost in their own happy alpaca world.

Cinderella had her mind on different matters. She was clearly agitated, alternately standing up and sitting down. She knew something was wrong, and so did I.

"I'll need to examine Cinderella, Jackie," I said. "We'll soon find out what's going on, don't worry. Can you steady her head?"

"Of course. And I've got some warm water ready for you," she replied.

I readied myself to investigate. Jackie stroked the alpaca's neck and talked calmly and quietly, offering constant reassurances. I couldn't hear exactly what she was saying, but Cinderella seemed to be replying to her every word. Maybe they were both speaking "alpaca"?

Meanwhile, at the other end, I advanced my hand gently, wiggling it from side to side to try and work out what was going on. Before long, I couldn't move my hand forwards any more. It was as if I'd pushed my hand into the depths of a trouser pocket or the end of a sock. I couldn't move it any further, but I couldn't touch the baby either. Could this be correct? I tried again, but I still couldn't feel the baby.

This could mean only one thing – Cinderella had a serious condition where the lining had twisted around the cria, like the end of a sweet wrapper. It's a rare problem and one that means the baby has no chance of being born naturally. I had to act fast, but first I relayed my findings to Jackie, who was looking anxious.

"Jackie, it's even worse than last time," I explained gravely. "The womb has twisted. I'll need to do an emergency operation to get Cinderella's baby out safely."

Jackie's face fell. "I can't believe it!" she said, but I quickly reassured her that everything would be all right, provided the procedure went as I hoped it would. I was concerned for Cinderella, but also excited, because this would be a big challenge, and I like a challenge – it's not every day you get the chance to operate on an alpaca!

"We'll need to get Cinderella into that pen," I said, pointing to the corner of the shed. "I'll operate on her left side. Once it's untwisted, I should be able to get the cria out, then stitch everything back together again. Don't worry, Cinderella won't feel a thing because her side will be numbed with local anaesthetic."

"You make it sound so simple,"
Jackie replied.

It did sound simple, and it might be if
everything went to plan. I'd operated on
cows and countless sheep, but this was
unfamiliar territory for me. But I didn't
want Jackie to pick up on any nerves or
worries I might have, so I kept up the
light-hearted conversation.

"We'll be fine," I said. "Now, let's move
her to a safe spot."

We positioned Cinderella against the gate
and I gently clipped the thick fleece from her
side. It was as deep as a new carpet, and I felt
bad trimming it away. Alpaca fleece is the
softest and warmest fleece of all animals, and
does a great job at keeping them nice and
cosy. *At least it isn't cold outside*, I thought.

I scrubbed Cinderella's side with
antiseptic and cotton wool to make sure it

was clean, then dowsed it in surgical spirit to ensure everything was sterile. It must have tickled because she started fidgeting, but once I'd injected the anaesthetic, everything went numb and Cinderella seemed much calmer.

I organized my surgical kit on a sterile stainless-steel tray and knelt down next to her. I felt as if I should start by saying a prayer, but instead I took a deep breath and then exhaled noisily. Once surgery was under way, I became engrossed by the process and focused completely on the job in hand. My nerves vanished.

Jackie's nerves, however, had not vanished, but she spoke to Cinderella the entire time. "Well done, Cinderella. You're doing so well… You're very brave… Julian's nearly finished – soon we'll have a new baby for you." Cinderella replied in short sentences of alpaca.

It didn't take long to make good progress. I breathed a sigh of relief. Thank goodness Cinderella couldn't feel anything and would hardly react to my manoeuvres.

But Cinderella was naturally curious, and today, with her long neck, she did react. Not by jumping or trying to escape, but by gently turning her head to peer at what was going on. She blinked and fluttered her long eyelashes, staring with quiet astonishment in her huge, dark eyes.

What on Esarth is going on? she must have been thinking to herself as she blinked again. But it was only when I managed to unravel the cria and coax it into the fresh air that she was really taken by surprise! The amazed alpaca started making delighted squeals of joy and excitement as she saw her baby. I lifted out the newborn and laid it on the straw next to her. It was all very unusual and

I wasn't surprised to see that Cinderella was taken aback.

"Look at that!" exclaimed Jackie. "She's actually watching what you're doing! I know alpacas are curious creatures, but I can't believe it! I think she's impressed!"

I was busy attending to Cinderella, so Jackie moved the baby nearer to Cinderella's head. Usually, mothers develop an immediate close bond with a newborn, but Cinderella continued to focus on what I was doing. Occasionally she'd make contented noises of apparent approval – "Yes, that does look neat," she seemed to say, in alpaca-speak.

After her initial rush of enthusiasm at the appearance of her little cria, Cinderella showed very little interest in her new baby. In the excitement of the moment, I thought that Cinderella was just distracted by my work as I cleaned up her side.

The baby was on her feet by the time the final stitch had been placed and I stood back to admire my work.

A long row of small stitches in the middle of a large, square bald patch was the only sign of surgery. A wobbly cria was a welcome addition to the farm. I smiled widely as she tottered around, looking for her first meal.

"Isn't it amazing how a new baby always knows exactly where to find milk?" Jackie said, wondering at the miracle of new life. We'd all done well this afternoon and the outcome couldn't have been better.

I cleaned up the mess that I'd made, washed my hands, arms and face, then hosed down my waterproof trousers and wellies. Finally, I said my farewells to Cinderella and her baby. I could have stayed all afternoon, but I was needed back at the practice, where there was certainly more work for me.

"You've done an amazing job," Jackie said out of the blue. "If this one had been a boy, I was going to call it Julian. But it's a girl, so I'll have to call it Julie. I hope that's OK with you?"

"It's a lovely name for a lovely alpaca and much more suitable than naming her after me!" I replied.

I was secretly pleased. I don't like it when farmers or pet owners name their animals after the vet. It always seemed to be the case that the calf called Julian is the one unfortunate enough to be accidentally squashed by its mother, or it's Julian the pig who gets stuck in a ditch. Naming an animal after me often leads to disaster!

At least, with a name like Julie, my newest delivery stood a better chance of getting off to a good start in life. At least that was what I hoped…

A few days later, Emmy and I called back at the farm to check on the progress of Cinderella and her baby. Jackie was in the field when I arrived. Cinderella had her head down, munching grass. Julie was happily cuddled under Jackie's arm.

That's odd, I thought. Normally, babies don't leave their mother's side.

Jackie waved me over. She was clutching a huge plastic bottle with a rubber teat on the end. As I got closer, I could see Julie was dribbling frothy milk from the corners of her mouth.

"How are Mum and baby?" I asked from one side of the fence.

"Both doing really well. Cinderella is pretty much back to normal. The stitches look neat and everything is healing nicely. You'd hardly notice she'd had an operation at all! Julie is doing very well too, but I'm having to top her up with milk. Mum hasn't got very much and she's not really interested in her."

This was a problem. The lack of milk can be managed by giving a young animal extra from a bottle. But if the mother doesn't bond with the baby, it can become an orphan, brought up and looked after by the other alpacas – or, in this case, a kind human being.

It's not ideal. Jackie knew this all too well.

It was an occasional complication associated with a surgical delivery, where some mothers don't even realize they've had a baby at all, and their maternal instincts don't develop. In Cinderella's case, the operation was unavoidable, but I hoped she would eventually form a family unit with Julie. I needed to leave it a little longer to see. I told Jackie that I'd come back in another week to take out Cinderella's stitches and I'd review the situation then. Jackie agreed and turned her attention back to Julie, who suckled happily at the bottle.

A week flew by and before long I was on my way back to Jackie's. My drive to the farm was filled with worry. Would Cinderella's instincts have kicked in? Could that bond, which should last a lifetime, have strengthened? Or would Julie be an orphan alpaca?

"Let's hope that Cinderella and Julie are back on track, eh?" I said to Emmy.

She looked up at me as if to say, "Who are Cinderella and Julie?"

Jackie was her usual cheerful self when I arrived, despite looking exhausted.

"Morning, Julian!" she called. "Look at little Julie. Not so little now!"

"My word! She's grown a lot ," I commented. The youngster had developed a fluffy white fleece and looked like a poodle, or a pile of neatly stacked cotton-wool balls, on long, sticklike legs. She looked happy, strong and healthy, making non-stop squeaks and shrills – the sounds of a contented alpaca.

"But I've been feeding her every two hours, day and night. I'm exhausted," Jackie said with a weary smile. "It's been hard work but worth it. The problem is, Julie thinks I'm her mum now! She follows me everywhere, especially when I've got the bottle of milk. Her mother doesn't realize she has a baby and Julie doesn't recognize her as a mother. It's all a bit topsy-turvy, but it seems to be working out OK."

Cinderella was waiting impatiently in the same pen, staring out to the field where her alpaca friends were waiting. I needed to check her over and remove her stitches but she didn't want to be captured. Obviously Cinderella recognized me as the strange man who had made her side numb and tingly, then had deposited a strange and gangly creature in front of her. She didn't want to make my acquaintance again, and ran wildly in circles, avoiding capture and making very bad-tempered noises.

Finally, Jackie took hold of her head collar and held her still. The wound looked excellent – clean and healed. Taking out the stitches didn't hurt at all, but Cinderella was already fed up with my presence and got her revenge by spitting a huge mouthful of stinky, chewed-up grass in my direction. It sprayed my face and splattered my hair. While this was quite disgusting, it was an occupational hazard when working with alpacas. They're good at spitting and good at aiming!

It's one way an alpaca shows that it's annoyed. Spluttering to clear my face, I didn't take too much offence.

"Shall we try again then, Cinderella?" I said, quickly wiping away the green goo.

She didn't like it when I checked her udder either. The hard, empty area confirmed that she had no milk to give to Julie.

"There's nothing there at all, is there, Jackie?" I said, confirming the fact that no milk had developed.

"No, and she's still showing no interest in her baby. She'd rather eat grass and hang out with her alpaca friends," Jackie replied. "But it doesn't matter," she went on as she ruffled the fleece on Julie's neck again. "I'm her mum now – at least that's what she thinks. And I'm sure she even thinks she's a human!"

We opened the gate and, demonstrating the truth of what Jackie had just said, Cinderella trotted out into the paddock to rejoin the rest of the herd.

As I left the farm, I couldn't help but wonder how Julie would cope as she grew. Even at just a few weeks old, she'd had a challenging start to life. A touch-and-go birth, a mother with no milk, and already an identity crisis that crossed species! But one thing for sure was that she and Jackie had formed a special bond. She was lucky to have found another such caring mother.

Some weeks later, on a sunny afternoon, I was back to treat another alpaca at Jackie's farm. This one had a sore leg and I needed to give it an injection. It was a simple procedure, but one that had to go smoothly so as not to introduce any infection. The patient, and a few other alpacas, had been corralled into a small collecting pen prior to my arrival, so it would be easy to catch.

In the group of five or six creatures, a familiar fluffy face stood out from the others. It was Julie! She didn't need an examination or any treatment, but evidently liked to be part of the action.

"Do you recognize this one?" Jackie asked, nodding in Julie's direction.

"Of course I do! How is she getting on? Does she still think she's a human?" I had so many questions about the alpaca I had delivered into the world.

Jackie laughed. "Oh no, she's definitely an alpaca! She's the bossy one who's always the centre of attention! She's already the leader of the alpaca pack."

I laughed too. "That's great! I'm so glad Julie has found a home in the field, and not in your house."

I finished checking over the rest of the herd before we let them back into the field.

The sun was setting as I fetched Emmy. Together we stood just behind a low stone wall, happily watching the herd grazing.

It had been a busy few months. The weather conditions had been harsh, and often difficult to work in, but there was also something beautiful about wintertime in this very special part of the world.

I smiled as I remembered all the farms, farmers and animals that I'd visited. I'd brought lambs and calves into the world. I'd been outwitted by a wild kitten, chased a chatty parakeet around the practice and even swung an alpaca through the air! It had been quite a start to my time as a vet.

I looked at Emmy and beckoned her to come. She wagged her tail happily and we set off together. I couldn't wait to find out what adventures the rest of the year had in store for us.

ABOUT THE AUTHOR

JULIAN NORTON is a respected
veterinary surgeon, regular on
the best-loved series *The
Yorkshire Vet* and author
of many novels for adults,
including *Horses, Heifers and
Hairy Pigs: The Life of a Yorkshire
Vet* and *All Creatures: Heart-Warming Tales
from a Yorkshire Vet*. Having worked in Yorkshire
at various animal practices, he became a partner
at a practice at which Alf Wight (better known
under his pseudonym of James Herriot) worked. In
2019, Julian set up Sandbeck Veterinary Centre in
Wetherby. He also spends a lot of time working in
Thirsk, a town that he has made his home. Julian
continues to appear on *The Yorkshire Vet* as well as
regularly appearing as a guest on television shows
and literary events. *Adventures with a Yorkshire Vet:
Lambing Time and Other Animal Tales* is Julian's first
collection of animal stories for children. This will
be followed by his second collection, *The Lucky Foal
and Other Animal Tales*.

ACKNOWLEDGEMENTS

My first children's book has been a lot of fun
to write and also challenging. I'm so grateful to
Walker Books and Sophie and David at MBA
Literary Agents for encouraging me so vigorously
to write this book. Sarah Handley and Charlie
Wilson have given me huge support in this
project and so has Anne, my long-suffering wife,
who is also a vet. Anne has helped with edits
and comments throughout my writing. Louise
Jackson's art direction has guided the creation
of this beautiful book. Jo Weaver has added her
wonderful drawings on the cover and inside, on
the pages, and I love the way she has brought my
animal stories to life – I hope you agree! Finally,
as promised, my heartfelt thanks must go to the
staff of The Mockingbird Deli in the small town of
Yarm in North Yorkshire, purveyors of the finest
coffee and delicious sustenance. Many of these
stories have been remembered and collated into
this book inside their wonderful little cafe.